PRAISE FOR HANG ON TIGHT!

In *Hang on Tight!*, Suzanne Moore eloquently touches on the secrets to entrepreneurial success: setting expectations, work ethic, confidence, just enough (but not too much) ego, and bravery. I have built a successful business and attribute much of that to learning to be fearless—even when I felt fearful—and to surrounding myself with the right people. Her metaphor of entrepreneurship as a roller coaster is spot on. My favorite quote from the book, "When you step onto a roller coaster, you can't expect to get a train ride." BOOM! Mic Drop! I will be sharing that with my clients for years to come!

— KASEY ANTON, FOUNDER / CEO SPARK BUSINESS CONSULTING

In *Hang on Tight!*, Suzanne Tregenza Moore not only imparts valuable entrepreneurial wisdom but intertwines imperative life lessons as well. Her ability to apply these life lessons to the roller coaster ride of entrepreneurship makes this book both a practical guide and a joy to read! Whether you are holding on for dear life to your business, or white knuckling through life, this book is for you, so buy your ticket and get on board!

— NICOLETTE BLANCO, AUTHOR, *BY A THREAD: RESILIENCE STRATEGIES FOR THE PARTIALLY UNRAVELED*

Hang on Tight! is the book I wish I had when I started my entrepreneurial journey because it would have forewarned me about the many ups and downs I was about to encounter. Thankfully, Suzanne Tregenza Moore wrote this book now so not one more woman entrepreneur will wonder if she's normal for being scared, or uncomfortable, or for feeling 'less than.' Filled with Suzanne's lessons, you will love her candor and storytelling. *Hang on Tight!* is like having the wisest business mentor right in the palm of your hands.

— JILL CELESTE AUTHOR, *LOUD WOMAN: GOOD-BYE, INNER GOOD GIRL!*

Suzanne is a courageous, generous, and authentic leader who changes lives every day. Her impactful and priceless guidance to other entrepreneurs through her book, *Hang on Tight!*, will undoubtedly supply them with strategies, support, and inspiration to drastically move the needle in their pursuit of happiness and success. This extraordinary work is not to be missed. WOW, Suzanne, what a gift to the world!

— SHANNON CROTTY, FOUNDER/CEO POLKA DOT POWERHOUSE

As Suzanne Moore states being an entrepreneur is a roller coaster ride that will have you screaming in terror or laughing with exhilaration—frequently, you will be doing both simultaneously. *Hang on Tight!* reminds you that you aren't alone, gives you questions to help you understand, and steps to improve, your experience. Looking for the perfect gift for an entrepreneur at any stage of the journey? This is it.

— JEN DRAPER, ENTREPRENEUR

Hang on Tight! is such an enjoyable book to read. It contains wisdom from Suzanne's own life and business. Her descriptions of what tries to stop us and how to move forward are relatable and instructional. Readers will find guidance and inspiration in these pages.

— Judy Kane, Founder, Aligned Consciousness

A fun, yet down-to-earth and practical book that every entrepreneur should read. The stories are so relatable, you barely realize there's a lesson being taught until you find yourself saying, "Ah ha. Yes, exactly!"

— Dawn McGee, Nutrition Evangelist, DawnMcGee.guru

Suzanne uses charming stories and relatable examples to guide the reader through valuable lessons we can all apply to our businesses and our lives.

— Connie Jo Miller, Owner,
Enigma Bookkeeping Solutions

Having spent most of my work life in corporate, I had no idea what I was in for when I started my business. If you're thinking of starting a business, just getting started or questioning if you have what it takes to keep going, read this book! Suzanne is the real deal, a phenomenal coach and business owner who knows what it takes to grow, pivot, and thrive in business. This is the book I wish I'd read when I was getting started. My recommendation: read it, integrate it, and use it as a guide to support your business growth.

— Jeannie Spiro, Business Coach

What a ride! *Hang on Tight!* draws you in with an easy-to-read style and short chapters. The lessons can be used by entrepreneurs in any business or industry. While Suzanne focuses on women entrepreneurs, men will benefit from the knowledge gained by reading this book, too. The lessons are easy to incorporate. I highly recommend *Hang on Tight!* to business owners out there who need the reassurance that they aren't alone in their fear and that they can be successful entrepreneurs; they just need to wait out that 112 seconds of rollercoaster riding fear.

— MICHELLE TEAGUE, ENTREPRENEUR AND CEO OF
A TEAGUE OF YOUR OWN

Yes, entrepreneurship is a bumpy ride. Suzanne does an excellent job dissecting the various ups and downs entrepreneurs face on a regular basis, whether it's confronting fear of failure or the fear of wearing an orange jumpsuit. I appreciated her compelling story that brought out valuable lessons for us to learn. Thank you, Suzanne for writing this book and congratulations for not barfing on the roller coaster of entrepreneurship!

— ELAINE TURSO, CHIEF VISIONARY PARTNER, INSOURCE IT
MARKETING AGENCY HTTPS://WWW.
INSOURCEITMARKETING.COM/

Hang on Tight! Learn to Love the Roller Coaster of Entrepreneurship bravely recounts the development of Suzanne Moore's relationship with fear, and the impact of that relationship on her life and business. Her vulnerability and wisdom about her own journey inspire entrepreneurs to explore our own and to identify where we sabotage our own growth. She offers valuable questions and advice to guide us through this process. While unlike Suzanne, I do not enjoy actual roller coasters, I have experienced no better way than entrepreneurship to accelerate my own personal and professional growth. I highly recommend this upbeat guidebook to anyone considering taking the plunge or already in the waters. *Hang on Tight!* will help you identify the patterns that are holding you back from the success of your dreams.

— DEBRA A. WOOG, CRISIS NAVIGATION PARTNER

HANG ON TIGHT!

HANG ON TIGHT!

LEARN TO LOVE THE ROLLER COASTER OF ENTREPRENEURSHIP

SUZANNE TREGENZA MOORE

Edited by
DEBORAH KEVIN

HIGHLANDER
PRESS

Hang on Tight!
Copyright © 2021 Suzanne Tregenza Moore

ISBN: 978-1-7359333-9-9
Ebook ISBN: 978-1-7372638-0-7
Library of Congress Control Number: 2021916503

Published by Highlander Press
501 W. University Pkwy, Ste. B2
Baltimore, MD 21210

Cover design: Patricia Creedon
Cover art: Retrostar/Adobe Stock
Editor: Deborah Kevin
Author's photo credit: Jane Repetti Chang Photography

For Kevin, Stuart, and Walter.
I love you.

She believed she could so she did.

— R.S. Grey, Scoring Wilder

CONTENTS

CELEBRATE

FOREWORD

Suzanne and I met almost ten years before this book was published at an early December women's networking group. I was the speaker, sharing my personal experience of starting a radio show after the challenges of divorcing and losing my mother and sister. At the end of the meeting, Suzanne asked to have her picture taken with me. I remember telling her, "You're making me feel like a celebrity." She showed her marketing savvy even back then by sharing the photo on social media, and highlighting the meeting, my talk, and my radio show.

In the years since, we've worked on a number of projects together. Suzanne participated as a member of the *Change Your Attitude... Change Your Life* Life Strategists Team delivering her marketing know-how in one-minute segments on my shows for three and a half years. As part of the team, she also wrote for my digital magazine, *24 Seven,* expanding on her radio segments and giving my entrepreneurial listeners solid marketing strategies to implement in their businesses. Suzanne also contributed to a book I published in 2015, *KEYS TO A GOOD LIFE: Wisdom to Unlock Your Power Within*.

I know Suzanne to be a cheerleader of other entrepreneurs' businesses and mindset. She presented to other Life Strategist team members on marketing topics and assisted one in taking her business from almost six figures to multi-six figures through one-on-one coaching. The group benefited from her wisdom.

In the thirteen years I have been running my shows, *Change Your Attitude...Change Your Life* and now *Conversations with Joan,* I've interviewed hundreds of non-fiction writers including Deepak Chopra, Mel Robbins, and Rachel Hollis. Having read all of their corresponding books, I've come to the conclusion that those who are striving forward all share a similar message: You can overcome whatever challenges you are facing to live a happy, purposeful, and successful life.

Suzanne's MBA in marketing and entrepreneurship was evident from the strategic nature of the monthly segments she shared on my radio show. What I love about this book is that, in addition to her business savvy, it also shows her heart. Entrepreneurs know there are many strategies they can implement. But what is important to understand in order to succeed is how to handle a situation when a strategy fails or when faced with seemingly unsurmountable challenges. This book provides that guidance.

Joan and Suzanne, Believe Inspire Grow Meeting. December 2011.

In *Hang on Tight!,* Suzanne shares the fears she's experienced and how they influenced her career and entrepreneurial path. Self-employed women will see themselves in Suzanne's story, and they will learn to appreciate the ups, downs, and twists and turns that come from riding the roller coaster inherent in owning one's own business. Her vulnerably shared story of raising her children, moving throughout the northeast to follow her husband's career, and building her business through life's challenges, provides great wisdom, solid guidance, and it grants the permission to show yourself kindness along the way.

Joan Herrmann
Host & Executive Producer
Change Your Attitude...Change Your Life's
Conversations with Joan Radio Show
Publisher, *24/Seven Magazine*
www.CYACYL.COM

INTRODUCTION

If you have ever felt for a moment that you were failing in your business, you'll want to read this book. Fear of failure is a pain that many entrepreneurs, especially self-reliant women, feel all too often, and keep to themselves. We hide it, as though fear, concern, or stress may make us seem weak and incapable. We allow ourselves to believe that indecision, bad decisions, a lack of confidence, or not hitting each of our goals as set forth are personal failures instead of being completely normal for those of us who choose to ride the roller coaster called entrepreneurship.

When you step onto a roller coaster, you can't expect to get a train ride. The highs and dips are part of the deal you've made with yourself. They are inherent to the experience. Yet, many women entrepreneurs find these peaks and valleys emotionally crippling.

We all end up on roller coasters for different reasons. Sometimes, our child leads us through the turnstile onto a ride we would never choose ourselves. Sometimes, we think we are getting on a different kind of ride only to find ourselves at the front of the line for one we didn't sign up for. Sometimes, we are told that a particular roller coaster won't be a really intense ride and even a wimp could handle it, then learn differently once strapped in and feeling there is no way out.

One solution to avoid the roller coaster is to stop being an entrepreneur. Go back to the grind of working for someone else: on their time, in their space, without the freedom you have now tasted. You can be that person who sees the "last chance to escape" sign after ninety minutes in line and says, "This one looks too scary for me. I'm outta here!"

If you are anything like me, you have tasted too much freedom to be employable anymore. You know in your heart, that making your business work is the only way you will feel whole. You are too far-gone, listening to the click, click, clicking of the car on the rails as it ascends a hill, and you anticipate the whoosh of air and drop of your stomach that will come just after its pause at the top.

If any of this sounds familiar, this book is for you. It will show you that starting, shifting focus, getting side-tracked, having life get in the way, re-starting, and feeling the angst associated with all of it are just part of the ride. Along the way, this book will provide you with direction, support, reframing, and mindset lessons, which will help you accept the twists and turns. Most importantly, this book will show you that you are not alone, that the cars in front of you and behind you are filled with others taking the same ride and having their own experience with it.

I am one of the women on this crazy ride. After more than ten years as an entrepreneur, I still find myself feeling down at times, questioning whether I know enough, focused on retooling mistakes I've made. At times, I realize I've gotten lost on Facebook and can't remember what I meant to do there—and I'd only planned on whatever it was taking a moment. I have had launch failures, pushed the limits with email marketing, pushed too hard--or not hard enough--and cried because something I tried bombed worse than I could have imagined. I am not immune to any challenges you might be facing; I have simply found ways to counter-balance them more quickly, get myself back on track, boost my confidence and energy again, and keep going.

My coaching work allows me to walk alongside so many other women who struggle. They tell me, "I'm a disaster. I haven't done what I was supposed to. I'm so far behind," long before they share that they made multiple sales from a single email. They tell me, "I feel like I'm treading water," "I don't know what I'm doing," and "I'm not making any money," because these are the stories they have invented in their heads.

My experiences have taught me to step back, look at the bigger picture, and reframe for them what they could see in the mirror, rather than the image they are creating. My clients leave our sessions feeling grounded, clear on their next steps, and confident. My intention for you is that you will feel the same after reading this book.

Within, you will read about my many crazy life adventures and entrepreneurship journey. I'll tie them together to show you important lessons I've learned along the way.

I will cover:

- How fear shows up and can derail your plans and progress;
- Understanding the driving force within you that will keep you going even when times are hard;
- Why knowing your business values is crucial for your long-term success;
- The critical role that mindset plays on everything you do;
- That inner strength will be your saving grace when it seems everything has fallen apart;
- The different types of communities you need around you in order to create success;
- What leadership really is and what it isn't; and
- Why celebrating isn't an act of the ego.

Clients tell me that I share lessons succinctly. They appreciate that I don't drone on about topics. I get in and get out, leaving them with a clear picture of what they need to learn.

By the time you finish this book, you'll realize that whatever holds you back is as temporary as you allow it to be. You will trust that every up and down, twist and turn, and loop-de-loop your car on the roller coaster takes, will ultimately make you stronger. You will realize that acceptance is not weakness, but strength and perseverance are among

the best qualities an entrepreneur can have. You may even be entertained along the way.

I wish that someone had placed a book like this in my hands ten
years ago. I also wish I could turn back the clock and take all the
energy I spent feeling like a failure and put it into serving others. If I
could, I can't imagine what my business would look like today.

Don't make the same mistakes I did. Choose to make today the day
you see yourself as part of a larger community of women entrepreneurs. Find within these pages whatever you need in order to be okay
with where you are right now and to take the next step on your ride.
The track is in front of you. You just need to strap in and hang on tight!

FEAR

1

FEAR

Fear is universal and comes from a time when we needed it to
remain safe from animals and other tribes wishing to harm us.
My dog reminds me often how instinctual fear is when she shies away
from my reach. She is an animal who has never experienced any harm,
yet her diminutive size and instinct tell her to "watch out" when I
move too quickly toward her.

Roller coasters elicit fear in us. They create anticipation, and then
shock our bodies through twists, turns, and the centrifugal force
needed to hold the cars to the track even when upside-down. Entrepreneurship, in its own way, does the same. It builds anticipation, turns
without warning, and shocks the system.

There are many types of fear that can hold us back. I have found naming them and knowing which ones I am most likely to succumb to helps me from getting ensnared.

2

THE SWING

I have always been a night owl and a great sleeper. My husband
envies my ability to go back to sleep in the morning and gets frustrated that I can easily sleep until ten or eleven on a weekend morning.
Fortunately, as our children shift to their teenage years, he hasn't been
quite as surly about it. Because of my night owl tendencies, it's
unusual for me to rise early.

But one morning when I was seven years old, my eyes popped
open at sunrise on Silver Lake during our first full summer at our
newly renovated New Hampshire vacation home. The strangeness of
feeling alone in the house wafted over me. I crept down the stairs from
the loft bedroom I shared with my brother doing my best not to wake
him. Arriving in the living room, I considered turning the television
on, but remembered there were only three channels at the lake and I
would have to turn the antenna to see what was on. Knowing the
sound might wake my parents, I decided against television.

Instead, I walked through the galley kitchen and stepped out onto
the back stoop, checking to see if Geoffrey the chipmunk was ready for
a morning peanut. He was nowhere to be found. Turning back toward
the lake, I watched the sun rise over the hill across the water. I walked

toward the lake front side of the house and to "my swing." Dad had just installed a swing beneath the deck that ran along the front windows of our walkout basement. It had a simple brown, wooden seat, stained to match the house siding and hung from two large, braided ropes so new that they squeaked a little with each pass. While everyone was welcomed to use it, the swing felt like mine.

Quietly, so as to not awaken my family, I started swinging, lightly at first, but soon I was seeing how high I could get. I swung for a while then chose to dismount classically, jumping when the swing was at its apex, landing hard, and running a few steps across the somewhat rough, recently hardened cement, my momentum carrying me forward.

As I came to a stop, I noticed an enormous black water snake slithering across my path under the shade of the deck. One more step and my foot would have collided with it. I screamed!

At one time, Silver Lake was called Six Mile Pond because its perimeter measured six miles. My scream—which likely measured over one hundred decibels on any reasonably calibrated noise level-o-meter—magnified by the water, surely reached every home on the shoreline that morning. I felt paralyzed by fear as I stared down at the snake. Mental calculations and questions flooded my brain. If I ran away, would it slither after me? Could I safely make it to the lawn or the basement door? No direction seemed safe for a successful escape.

Needless to say, it wasn't very long before my parents arrived and attempted to calm me. The snake took its leave, seemingly happy to remove itself from the intruders who had interrupted its morning. Neighbors popped into our front yard to ensure that all was well, giggling as they learned the cause of the raucous.

Remembering this story as I write it, I'm struck by what remains to this day: fear. I was fully paralyzed by it, unable to move in any direction, screaming and screaming. It is the only time in my life I've stood still and screamed like that; however, it wasn't the last time fear would paralyze me. As an adult, looking back on this moment, I see how fear, my own and that of others, affected my choices, and my path.

Fear, communicated to me as love and concern, acted as a catalyst to my decisions. While I'm tempted to wonder what my path might have looked like if I'd simply stepped around the proverbial snake each time it appeared in front of me, I choose to see that each moment helped me become the person I am today.

3

FLORESCENT LEGGINGS AND CHOCOLATE CAKE

I grew up in suburban New Jersey about forty-five minutes west of Manhattan. My dad commuted into New York City until I was about eleven, returning home every evening smelling like newsprint. That's when he left his investment-banking job in the city to start his own, independent investment-banking firm, doing so for two primary reasons: he didn't like commuting, and he wanted to be able to spend the entire summer at our recently renovated lake house. He told me many times that working for someone else didn't allow you to be in charge of your own destiny or success. He believed that being self-employed was the most likely path to both financial and personal freedom. I'm sure I get my entrepreneurial spirit from him; if not, certainly my desire for freedom.

My childhood was fairly idyllic by any standards. My parents loved each other and made me feel loved. I had everything I needed—and most of what I wanted. My older brother completed our family of four along with our two cats, Butterfly and Whiskers.

Our network of friends included business leaders, philanthropists, and involved mothers. As fantastic as these folks were, they appeared extremely homogeneous. When we become adults, we realize that while we have been shaped by our surroundings, there are many different ways to be, dress, think, or live. As a child, we know only what we've seen. I witnessed many people who made choices similar to those around them. They dressed the same, discussed the same things at parties, sent their children to a short list of private schools, and drove similar cars.

Both my parents were conservative, moderately preppy, and well appointed—just like all my friends' parents were. My mother—it seemed to me—naturally fit into our world. She looked much like all the other moms I knew. Slim, put together, well dressed; even her sweat suits matched. I don't ever remember her leaving the house without make-up and her hair perfectly styled. My father rarely left the property in New Jersey without a sport coat and tie, even on the weekends. It never occurred to me that others in the world lived differently. Back then, I viewed "different" as negative, other, an outlier —unwelcome.

As a result, I wanted to fit in. Fitting in felt extremely important to me, and I can look back now and see how I would have been much happier if it hadn't. (Ah, the things we wish we could tell ourselves earlier in life, right?)

Like many teens, I felt insecure and wanted everyone to like me. I wanted to be invited to every party. Friends got certain types of clothing and I immediately wanted the same. Having a Benetton sweatshirt and Guess jeans or L.L. Bean boots seemed all-important. Girls who displayed apparent confidence drew me to them like a moth to a flame. Of course, that was usually how I ended up getting burned.

Occasionally, outside cultures influenced my interests. I explored dressing in more modern and popstar-inspired fashion despite *The Official Preppy Handbook* being the guide most of my contemporaries seemed drawn to. I let my grandmother perm my hair to create body and sprayed it with copious amounts of Aqua-Net in an attempt to make it look more voluminous. I remember my father's quizzical expression at some of my outfits and my mother supportively saying, "It's what the kids are wearing." Despite this, my never-owned-a-pair-of-jeans-in-his-life father did not understand the value of fluorescent leggings or an armful of jelly bracelets.

The fit-in vibe was reinforced by the private schools I attended, the

clubs my parents joined, and the friends I chose. What I didn't understand then was that when everyone tries to fit in, there's incredible
pressure to not be seen as different.

I was different though, and as I grew into my teenaged years,
those differences started to become more evident to me. I loved
being involved in the school theater program rather than participating in the more prestigious field hockey and lacrosse teams.
Unlike the traditional surly teenager who learns to loath most adults,
I loved the extracurricular conversations I had with teachers, school
administrators and my friends' parents. Most of the time, I even got
along with my own parents; likely the result of the fact that I wasn't
trying to get away with something that would have gotten me in
trouble.

By the time I was fifteen, I started to find the version of myself that
was comfortable in my homogenous culture but could also express
myself authentically. I chose the activities that lit me up. I befriended
others whose self-expression was evident in the activities they chose,
the clothing they wore and the relationships they formed. My pack
became the less-popular theater geeks, a group of people who seemed
more interested in finding the outer edge of our homogenous culture
while not eschewing it completely.

I give my parents a lot of credit for the fact that, despite the
uniform society I was growing up in, I was able to develop my own
sense of self. My mother's upbringing had been extremely strict, and
she expressed to me that she wanted me to feel more freedom than she
had. My dad, simply put, treated me like I could do anything. Of
course, he envisioned a very traditional future for me, but he always
supported me and offered encouraging words.

Also, by fifteen, I'd stopped growing and begun maturing physically. With this shift a lifelong conflict began with my mother. It started
with comments like, "you're looking fluffy and you need to watch
what you are eating," or, "you would have such a lovely figure if you
would only…" I weighed one hundred and sixteen pounds when this
began. Having maintained her weight well below that for years
however, my mother gave me the impression she felt my weight was
really going off the rails. Mom and I remain close in many ways, but

this is one area in which we have struggled. Mom tried to keep me from eating; as a result, I ate more.

I remember coming home from college with some girlfriends. My parents were always happy to have me, and any friends I wanted to bring around. Knowing that we were coming, they planned a nice dinner and mom made a chocolate cake for dessert. She served to my friends and father regular slices of cake, but a paper-thin sliver landed on my plate. (To this day, my friends and I laugh about the comedic aspect of my serving being a quarter of theirs).

Over the years, the similar slights, the sideways glances at my self-apportioned plate, the shocked expression over something I might choose to eat, laid bare my mother's disapproval, which angered me beyond measure. They robbed me of the opportunity to create my own sense of my body and how I felt about it. Or to create my own sense of the food I ate, and how I felt about it. Innately, I felt the need to defend my choices rather than to examine them.

I've worked for years to not hear my mother's critical voice in my head when I look at food. I earned a health coaching degree. I've spoken to psychotherapists, and I've even worked with a PSYCH-K® facilitator who helped me to transform my sub-conscious beliefs around health and my body.

Through these experiences, I've learned that my mother's issue really had nothing to do with me. I believe she suffers with perfectionism that comes from her own rigid upbringing. She carries her own demons, not just around weight, but also her surroundings: what they should look like and whether they are worthy. These demons live in her head, and, from my perspective, they never leave her alone.

For the most part, I've accepted that mom's obsession with every morsel of food she ingests is hers. Her choice to chastise herself after each meal is hers, too. While I don't want to live that way, I'm not living her life, and I need to let her do her.

Looking back at the many times I was told how beautiful my mother was, or looked on a given evening, I'm saddened for her. I hope on all those occasions she felt as beautiful as she was. While she might have felt some of it, my sense is that it was overshadowed by what she sees as her imperfections.

Despite spending many years deeply angry at my mom for her obsession with my body, I realize now that my sense of self was strengthened by it. The combination of her supporting me by being more relaxed than her own parents and her perfectionism contributed to me paving my own path despite the pressures I experienced. While I consider myself a recovering perfectionist, I know that its hold over me never paralyzed me as much as it could have.

I marvel now at the symbolism of my mother, directly and indirectly, encouraging me to be smaller. Consciously, I believe she wants me to achieve all I am capable of. Sub-consciously, I believe her perfectionism keeps her in a state of fear when she sees me put myself "out there" imperfectly. This isn't about her conscious desire for me to be small. I believe it is her sub-conscious fear of what might happen to me if I am not. It is too deeply ingrained in her that we can only be happy, or fully realize achievement, if we look "right" on the outside—if we are perfect in the eyes of others. What I've learned from this experience, and so many others, is that when someone tries to keep you small—in any way—it is usually because of their own discomfort with what you are doing.

Perfectionism is the ultimate form of fear. Perfectionists keep themselves from moving forward by focusing on what is not yet done, not yet ready. It is easy for any one of us to see what is wrong with anything we are about to put out into the world. The challenge is that too often the focus on what is wrong keeps us from sharing all that is right. It holds us back from taking our next step, and as a result from growing by taking that next step.

Conversely when we take the step, release the program, get on the stage, take up the space we want to, we learn from the experience. It enriches us. We take the learning and improve. This is why there are updates, versions 2.7, and fourth editions. Nothing is ever perfect; at some point, it just has to be good enough.

My senior year of high school, I had the lead in the spring musical, *The Robber Bridegroom*. The first night, at the very beginning of the show, the music vamped and I jogged gingerly out to a platform that had been constructed to bring me beyond the boundaries of the proscenium into the audience. I belted out the lyrics of two stanzas, setting the scene for the entire show. At the end of the second stanza, the audience briefly erupted signaling their appreciation, then quieted as the show continued. I felt triumphant at their applause. The second night, I repeated the first stanza instead of singing the second. After a line or two, I realized that I'd just bungled the top of the show. Panic rose within me, as I knew this meant the audience wouldn't understand the back-story my lines, when delivered correctly, told. I glanced over at my teacher, enthusiastically banging away on the piano. His eyes sent me the message that the show must go on. This wasn't the dress rehearsal, and imperfect had to be good enough.

I carry this lesson with me in all that I create for my business. I know that without deadlines, I am lost. It is why I'm committed to delivering content at the same time every week. It is just as easy for me to allow time to slip by as I noodle over a script as it is for anyone else. Instead, I generally give myself no more than thirty minutes to write them and move forward with what I have. At some point, the show must go on, and there is no space left for perfectionism.

4

NO ORANGE JUMP SUIT

Halfway through middle school, I switched schools. While most students transitioned to the private schools in my area either at the start of seventh or ninth grade, I moved in eighth. One of my dearest friends had transitioned in seventh, as was her family tradition, and I begged my parents to let me go the year after, excited to be with her and settled for high school. I began that year with such excitement, but my struggles began shortly into the school year.

I accepted the invitation to go out with several girls for Halloween. I expected to trick-or-treat, anticipating filling a bag with delicious goodies. The other girls had different ideas. Instead, I found myself in the woods watching the others experiment with cigarettes wondering if our group would set fire to the dried autumn leaves. My discomfort did not go unnoticed, and the following week I began to be shunned by the group. This commenced my lessons in thirteen-year-old girls being vicious to each other.

From that day on, I was an outcast. My clothes weren't cool enough. My shoes were old lady shoes. When I compared myself as having a similar look to one of the other girls noting our freckles and light hair, she looked disgusted that there could be any similarity.

Between hormones, social adjustments, and all-around insecurity, my experience of thirteen-year-old-girls is that they often behave like the nastiest humans on the planet. I have said for many years that you couldn't give me a million dollars a year to teach a room full of them. God bless the middle school teachers of the world!

In addition to the social and emotional challenges I faced that year, there were some academic ones. In prior years, math had been a strength for me. My placement in honors algebra seemed obvious when developing my schedule for my first year at the new school. Oh man, I really struggled through that class.

I hated my math teacher for most of eighth grade. She had a thick German accent and high expectations of her students. Between the accent and struggling with the pace of the class, I found myself in self-inflicted victimization. I blamed the teacher for my struggles. It wasn't until I started to see her as my ally in getting through the course, rather than as the enemy, that I began to turn things around academically. Once I made this necessary mindset shift, I recognized her as the caring and supportive human being she was.

What I didn't know that first year, was that by luck, I ended up having Mrs. Schlüter for math four out of my five years at the school. By my senior year, in addition to being teacher and student, we were friends. I prioritized my work for her class, and I excelled in it, enjoying the challenge of calculus.

My favorite story about her is from my senior year. She was my academic advisor, so I often found myself with her discussing my academic workload and extracurricular activities. This is where I was early in the week of the spring musical in which I was playing the lead. That week we would also complete a chapter in our calculus text. Our years together taught me patterns in her teaching, and I knew she had something up her sleeve.

Our conversation went something like this, "Okay, Mrs. Schlüter, I know we're having a pop quiz this week, and I really have a lot going on! I just need to know whether it is going to be Thursday or Friday?"

I'll never forget the glint in her eye when she looked at me and responded in her German accent, "Well, it's not Friday." It makes me giggle to this day that she let me in on her secret.

The trust between us was immense, which is why when I told her,

"I think I want to be a math teacher." I took her rapid and emphatic response deeply to heart.

"Don't do it," she exclaimed. "Be a civil engineer." A lot of adult reasons why becoming a civil engineer would be a better career for me followed. I found none of them compelling. I thought of myself in an orange jump suit on the side of a road with a tripod and immediately dismissed the civil engineer concept.

I know her reasoning came from the heart. I believe she was looking out for my earning potential and my ability to grow within a role without feeling pigeonholed. Looking back on our conversation, I also believe that she spoke from her own exhaustion and frustration with her job. There is no job that's perfect. We all struggle from time to time with the paths that we've chosen. In those moments it is typical to warn others not to follow our path.

Her warning came from genuine care and concern for me. She didn't want to see me unhappy and felt I would be if I pursued becoming a teacher. She was likely right. I think if I'd chosen the path of teacher, it would not have been a long-term career for me. You read my earlier comments about teaching thirteen-year-old girls, right? However, I also know that I let my fear of the unknown, not understanding what other jobs related to math there might be, keep me from pursuing it.

Fear of the unknown strikes in so many ways. Any time we try something new, or even consider trying something new, it can rear its ugly head and paralyze us from moving forward. This happened for me with a math career and has happened so many subsequent times with initiatives in my own business. I recall courses I intended to create, webinars I wanted to run, and groups I wanted to lead none of which came to fruition because something about them was new and unknown to me. Each idea I didn't act on could have been the one that catapulted my success. Of course, it could also have ended in abject failure. I'll never know. Either way, I missed out on the learning and the experience because I didn't try. Instead, I let the fear of the unknown paralyze me.

What I've learned is when attempting to do something I've never done before I am much more likely to accomplish my goal when I connect with someone who is a step or two ahead of me. Everything seems difficult, strange, and impossible until we've done it. Then the mystery is solved, and it just doesn't seem so hard anymore.

If I'd been more open, as a senior in high school, to exploring a career in engineering, it's possible I may have found a career path that suited me, Perhaps what I needed was someone to expand my knowledge of the steps and possibilities. Although I am absolutely certain I would never have signed up for anything that put me in an orange jumpsuit.

5

TREGENZA

In high school, I developed an enduring love for theater. I had always liked to sing along to musicals and envision myself as the lead in *Annie, The King and I, Les Miserable*. Getting to actually perform on stage really lit me up.

I wondered if I could possibly make it as an actor. It didn't take much to dissuade me from this career path. Everyone will tell you how difficult a path acting is, how regularly rejected one feels. How hard it is to "make it" as an actor.

When I shared my thoughts about trying, no one in my life said, "Give it a whirl! You've got your whole life ahead of you! What do you have to lose?" Instead, fear, "It's a hard road." "You don't really want to do that, do you?" and my favorite, "You'll have to change your last name. Tregenza would be a horrible stage name."

I remember a conversation I had with my father about pursuing a career in acting. Uncharacteristically, he did not reassure me that I could accomplish anything I wanted. Instead, he told me how uncomfortable this path would make me. "Oh, Suzie," he said. "Why would you want to do that? People try for years to get acting jobs and end up waiting tables. You have so much potential to do anything you want, and you'll waste your time on something that probably won't ever happen." Dad made it clear to me that this path would make me uncomfortable.

It is true that most would-be actors don't find success, that they struggle hoping for an opportunity, that the level of rejection is not for the faint of heart. I took the advice of my dad and others, and chose a safer, more comfortable route, accepting that I would likely be one of the unlucky ones. What I learned much later is that achievements do not come from comfort. They come from accepting discomfort.

Let's consider this together: how many Olympic athletes do you think are selected to represent their countries at the games while staying in their comfort zone? I'm guessing none felt particularly comfortable through all the years of workouts and training, the early morning wake-up calls, and missing out on events with family and friends in order to be in top shape. I'm guessing none have commonly said, "I think I'll hang out with my friends this Saturday," when they were scheduled to be at a competition.

Instead, they made commitments to themselves, parents, coaches, and teams to do whatever it took to get to the Olympics. Comfort be damned. They worked their butts off to compete in their sport at an elite level, and to be better than all the other elites in their country.

This does not sound comfortable. In fact, it sounds really freaking hard. It sounds like something I would have approached with a lot of fear. In all likelihood, the same loving people in my life who told me, "It's a hard road," "you don't really want to do that, do you?" would have said the same about me becoming an elite athlete. Not because they didn't believe in me, but because they knew I'd need to get uncomfortable to achieve it.

Living in the comfort zone works for a lot of people. They do what's expected and reap rewards from it: stability, ease, a sense of peace and calm. There are many people for whom these rewards create richness in their lives. They are enough. These people are the steady trains who chug...chug...chug along next to those of us who love the fear and exhilaration of roller coasters.

The earlier in life we roller coasters realize that our passion and happiness lives outside of our comfort zone, the fewer regrets we will likely have. I did not understand this until my early forties. Internalizing it and living it came even later.

6

ALONE ON THE PHONE

Developing a fear of failure is common during the elementary school years as kids often face their first disappointments. That's when we begin to stop ourselves. Perhaps we don't want to read aloud in class for fear of making a mistake. Perhaps we don't try out for the school play or run for class president because we fear we won't be selected. Perhaps we don't get on the line for the roller coaster because a trusted adult says it could ruin our day. When we look back on our experiences and those of others, we can see choices that were made to avoid the pain of failure.

For many, this becomes a lifelong pattern. The fear of trying out for a sports team in high school becomes the fear of applying for the dream job after college and the fear of finding love in a marriage. Some individuals live their entire lives ensuring they never put themselves in a position to possibly fail.

Yet somehow, others find a way to push through their fear of failure. They ask a guy out even though they fear rejection, they apply for jobs they don't quite have the qualifications for on the chance they might be hired. They run the marathon, invest in the rental property, and move to a new city despite knowing no one, even when each choice seems crazy to others.

A few years ago, I met a woman named Melanie when she began attending a small-business networking group I'd started in Manchester, Vermont. She introduced herself as a life coach, but I learned she was also a professional skydiver. As we sat over coffee one day, she told me that, for some people, jumping out of a plane is easy, but the same person might be unable to dine in a restaurant alone, leave a bad marriage, or stand up to a boss. She explained that she loved working with people who were looking to bust through their fears no matter what they are. Jumping out of planes was not required.

Meeting Melanie gave me a new understanding of the fear of failure. Risk tolerance is different for everyone. No individual chooses one path or the other: always busting through fear or never confronting it. We all experience situations in which we are more willing to take a risk and others in which we cling to safety. However, as we grow, patterns emerge and, if we are not conscious of them, we tend to make more choices that belie our fears, rather than break through them.

Entrepreneurship ratchets up the importance of busting through our fear of failure. Leading a business requires countless large and small decisions every day. Every decision is another opportunity for triumph or failure. I've watched some women question each decision, and wither under the weight of them. I've watched others act decisively and fight like hell to ensure their choices work out. I've done both.

When I first started in business, a blog post or video took me days to create. I often sent them to friends for validation before sharing them publicly. I fretted over social media posts, feeling as though one wrong turn could make me or break me. Each decision seemed monumental and intimidating. I kept making them anyway.

One time in the first year of The Implementation Station, my virtual assistant business, I held a tele-class—that's how we connected before webinars. I dialed into the line early to be sure everything was working correctly. I had my script all ready, and the user interface on my computer open to the page where I would hit record. The top of the hour came, and I found myself alone on the phone line. I waited, hoping that registrants would join a moment late. Nothing.

As the seconds ticked by, I panicked and debated internally

whether to go ahead with my script or hang up and cry. Then, I remembered that I'd promised to send the recording to those who couldn't attend live, so I started reading through my script with gusto. At the end, I said something about thanking everyone for understanding that I had kept them muted for a clean recording. As promised, I sent that recording to all who registered and said nothing about the fact that I'd spoken, by myself, into the phone line until years later.

At around the same time, I developed a course I thought I could easily sell to ten or more people and instead got four or five to sign up. These experiences created a downward emotional spiral, a greater fear of failure and a lack of confidence. If this happened today, I would examine what went wrong with my marketing of each event. Whether better language could have been used, if I was getting in front of the correct audience. At the time, I chastised myself for being unable to get more people on the tele-class or enrolled in my course. Instead of choosing to learn from my experiences and to retool what didn't work, I chose to see these developments as confirmation my courses provided no value.

This lack of confidence led to struggles over small decisions, which, otherwise, should have been easy. Do I promote this again? Do I do some research on who connected and why and who didn't and why? The answer to both of these questions should have been an emphatic "yes!" Instead, during the struggles, my mind swirled things together and I questioned everything, "Was I foolish for thinking I knew enough to teach those courses? Maybe I tried to expand to courses too soon? Perhaps I should just stick to traditional virtual assistance and leave the courses to others who knew more?"

My roller coaster riding friends helped to pick me up and dust me off from these experiences. They reminded me that this was part of what I signed up for. They also reminded me that in eliminating possible failure, I eliminated possible success.

I moved forward, offered free and paid classes again, hired people on my team, and got beyond fearing each tiny decision. Trust me when I share there were plenty of failures along the way. There were also successes. I learned from both.

Looking back at that time, I see that identifying the pattern of the downward spiral and having my entrepreneurial friends there to help me out of it was critical to moving my business forward. They helped me to stop my swirling, unproductive thoughts and find my confidence again even after huge disappointments. Having the right community around me filled with women who understood me was pivotal. The other pivotal element came from the realization that despite the failures, I was still standing, and I'd learned from my mistakes.

At some point, every woman stops herself because of the fear of failure. For entrepreneurs to be successful, we have to learn to push ourselves through the fear. There isn't a person alive who hasn't experienced failure, and who hasn't stopped herself from doing something because of the fear of experiencing that pain again.

Like me, you will want to watch for your patterns. You'll notice certain challenges create your downward spirals. You will also see what gets you out of them. You might need something different than a pack of friends to lift you up. Perhaps journaling or meditating will be your salvation.

Sometimes the learning comes in the form of small improvements: increased marketing, better messaging, or an email with a slightly catchier subject line. Other times it comes in the form of great big failures. The failures themselves are painful. You will have them, and they will continue to hurt. But rising after one will show you how strong and capable you are.

7

PANIC BUTTON

No matter what kind of fear you might deal with, the universal way to stop yourself from pushing through it is hitting the panic button. This process looks different for everyone and can look different every time we do it. (Yes, most of us hit it many times, not just once!) Each time, we can convince ourselves that we are making the right decision, one that will help us to keep growing. We tell ourselves this lie because it relieves us from the fear engulfing us. It feels so good to allow ourselves to hit the button and reverse course. I know this because of how many times I've done it myself.

In early 2016, I decided it was time to write a book. I outlined it, dictated a large portion of it, and then had the recordings transcribed. The book's focus was supporting entrepreneurs in online businesses. Looking back, I completed about seventy to eighty percent of a solid first draft. Then I got distracted. A phone call came from a trusted entrepreneurial friend. She invited me to write a chapter in her compilation book, assuring me that it would make me a best-selling author. Despite believing I could achieve a best-seller with my book, I focused on her book instead of my own. I convinced myself that I would learn from the experience and apply that learning to my own book.

I felt honored to be invited into that project. I knew many of the other women who were a part of it, and I was delighted to be among them. It fed my childhood desire to fit into my community. As a result, I convinced myself that participating in this project would impact my business more quickly than finishing my book and publishing it. The title of the compilation book was *Inspiration for a Woman's Soul: Opening to Gratitude & Grace*, and my offering focused on my family's lake home, which at that time had just been sold. While I'm proud of "The Lake House," looking back I can see that the decision to be a part of the project was a way of hitting the panic button. I allowed my friend's book to be the excuse I used to hold myself back from my own. I'd stepped seventy to eighty percent of the way into the spotlight of being an author in my own right only to shrink backward. I'd hit the panic button, stopping myself in the midst of real progress.

I used the panic button as many entrepreneurs do. I convinced myself that the decision to remain smaller was in my best interest. I allowed myself to believe that there was something to be learned by being a part of the other book first. In doing so, I relieved myself of stress, fear, and discomfort in the moment. Long-term, however, I know the decision did not serve me best. Instead of experiencing whatever lessons I might have learned by moving through the challenge of launching my own book at that time, that moment of relief yielded to several years of frustration with myself for not pursuing that piece of my dream.

This is just one of many examples I could share with you from my experiences. Whether taking on an additional business because it looked like it would be an easy way to make side hustle income or telling myself that I couldn't network because I just didn't have the time, I've found many ways over the years to sabotage my growth. You likely have too.

Today, I know that hitting the panic button is a natural part of entrepreneurial development. We all do it. The lessons are to learn how to do it less frequently, to recognize it sooner, and to reverse course when we've done so.

Learning to recognize our fears is a lesson that comes over time with experience. It's like building a muscle, slowly and thoughtfully so that it will support you when needed. Sometimes the growth comes internally with our own recognition. Sometimes caring entrepreneurial friends point out that our decisions seem to be coming from our fear.

One of the most important things I've learned along the way is that all fears, no matter what kind or how they present themselves, are created in our heads, and are not real. The fear feels real to us, but the perceived outcome is just a story we tell ourselves.

I told myself the story that being part of the anthology would be better for my business. Since then, I have even convinced myself that there were benefits to never having published the first book. I convinced myself that it was hollow, a pile of information without richness or contextual meaning.

It's possible that an editor would have helped me sort out that book's challenges. It is also possible that I would have pushed just to publish it rather than taking the time to create something that stood out more. I'll never know, because I didn't finish it and it no longer feels like a project I want to complete.

Five more years in business and five more years of personal growth and maturity will show in this book. And, this time, I will not hit the panic button. This time, I have a team of women surrounding me, supporting me. If I approach the panic button, start to make an excuse, hold myself back, shrink to become one of many instead of standing fully in the spotlight, I know these women will push me forward. They will tell me that my story, my message, even just the simple completion of this goal, is important. They will keep me from disappointing myself. To hell with what everyone else thinks.

In the five years between the start of the last book and the start of this one, I've learned a lot about my relationship with the panic button. Like so many other entrepreneurs, I question myself, wondering if I really am the fraud that I feel I am because there are others who know more than me. At these times, having an emotional support team around me is what keeps me on track. When I am attempting to do something big, bold, and scary, my fellow roller coaster riders encourage me and remind me of the value that I bring to others, that my contributions matter.

I've also learned that I self-sabotage by getting involved in new projects before finishing something I've already started. (Perhaps it's my love for dogs that makes me so willing to be distracted by squirrels?) I've learned that to counter-balance this, I need to be crystal clear on my goals and to make decisions based on examining whether those goals will be helped or hindered by adding something to my plate. In being clear, I'm getting better at holding distractions at arms-length.

Being held accountable for my goals is important for me to achieve them. My extroverted personality is served by finding others to help hold me accountable. This is why you will often see me sharing on social media about what I'm doing and writing about it in my newsletter. These are passive ways I ask people to hold me accountable, but the potential embarrassment of not following through works wonders for me.

I ask to be held accountable in more active ways too. I participate in a mastermind, hire a coach, or become part of a formal accountability group or partnership. Each of these has worked very well for me and continues to do so. I do all of this because despite the work I have done building the muscle of moving beyond fear, I know there will be times I simply can't, or won't, if left to my own devices.

The panic button looks different for all of us, and at different times. It took me a long time to identify how I pushed it for myself, and likely you will find the same. Watch for your patterns. Identify them and learn what you need in order to get back on track quickly.

8

INTERNALIZE THIS SECTION

S ome believe that others aren't afraid, that they got to the point where they don't feel fear anymore. I'm sorry to tell you this isn't true. Fear is too engrained in our psychological make-up for us to outgrow it.

If you are walking the entrepreneurial path, understanding your fears and how they show up for you will be critical to finding success. You'll also want to identify your risk tolerance for stepping out of your comfort zone and just how far out you are willing to go. Whether you are a dyed-in-the-wool perfectionist, horrified of the unknown, can't stand the idea of discomfort, or fear failure more than anything, getting beyond any of it starts with identifying it, accepting it, and keeping yourself from hitting the panic button.

The average length of a roller coaster ride is one hundred and twelve seconds. Can you imagine how successful your business would be if you only experienced one hundred and twelve seconds of fear? Even if I only experienced one hundred and twelve seconds of fear a day, I think I'd be way ahead of the game! Yet, just like the panic that rises within us when we are about to take a big step in our business, the story we create about what could happen in those one hundred and twelve seconds can paralyze us from moving forward.

I hope you will learn to identify your fears and what you need to counter-balance them. Here are some questions to get you started:

- Does getting caught up in perfectionism affect your business progress? If so, what could you shift to change it?
- Does fear of the unknown hold you back from trying new things? How does this impact your business?
- How does the potential for discomfort impact your business decisions? Are you good at pushing yourself outside of your comfort zone? Or do you play it safe?
- When have you stopped yourself because of fear of failure? When have you pushed through your fear of failure? Can you identify a differentiating element that could help you push through more often in the future?
- When have you pressed the panic button? If faced with a similar set of circumstances, what would you do differently today?

WHY

9

WHY

 Don't underestimate the ripple effect of what you do.
These kinds of actions have toppled empires.

— Leila Janah

One of the most famous TED Talks, at least among entrepreneurs, is, "Start with Why: How Great Leaders Inspire," by Simon Sinek. When I first saw it ten years ago, it blew me away. The talk has been watched millions of times, and its underlying premise is that people don't buy what you do; they buy *why* you do it.

Understanding the *why* of your business is important for two reasons. The first is in keeping with Sinek's assertion that humans are emotional beings, and we connect to one another through those emotions. When people understand *why* you care about selling whatever it is you sell, from paperclips to coaching to airplane engines, they are more likely to buy from you. The second is that when you understand *why* you sell what you sell, you will keep going with it, even when hard times hit.

Spoiler alert: your *why* is not to make money. This is a shocking statement, I know. Stick with me. If the deepest *why* you can come up with is to make money, you will find yourself in disappointment and you will give up. I don't know an entrepreneur whose business made money from day one and never had a slump. Please get in touch with me and let me know if you are the outlier!

Assuming you aren't, let's go back to the idea of humans as emotional beings. When experiencing a slump in business, the obvious desire is to throw in the towel. I've thought many times about giving up my business and finding a job with a steady paycheck. If all I cared about was the money, I'm sure I would have. But years ago, I established my *why*. That *why* is what kept me going and kept me coming back to my business. My business is not just about me, and it is not just about making money. I'm going to guess that yours isn't either.

10

CITIES AND SKYSCRAPERS

I spent the fall semester of my junior year of college in London. One of the courses was ideal for a speech and theater major as we attended theater twice a week and were required to provide critical analyses about each show we saw. Pretty cushy, right?

I loved every minute of being in a big city and learning so much about London. I took myself to museums, wrote reams worth of letters to friends back home, and spent many lively nights in English pubs enjoying a pint.

One of my favorite things to do was to grab my A-to-Z map of the entire city and hop on a double-decker bus. Once on board, I climbed the spiral staircase and, when possible, took the front seat located directly above the driver. I felt as though I was driving the bus. I learned so much about London and its layout by following the bus route via my open map.

Often, I would get off the bus not knowing what was nearby and just start walking, discovering different areas and their personalities along the way. One time, I hopped off in the banking district, oriented myself to the Thames, and walked along the river to the Tower of London. Another time, I found myself at Trafalgar Square and decided to walk north, watching Londoners go about their business, until I tired of walking. Then I hopped on the London Tube system to find my way home to Swiss Cottage. These experiences solidified my love for cities and the adventures they hold within them.

Returning a few months later to a tiny college campus in upstate New York, my heart ached to be back in a city. I couldn't imagine spending another two semesters in what felt like the middle of nowhere. Instead, I decided to spend the fall of my senior year off-campus as well. This time, I applied to the American University Washington Semester Program. There were numerous areas of focus there, including government, law, etc. I chose journalism.

Off I went at the end of August to Washington, DC, delighted to find myself in yet another unfamiliar urban area to explore. Before arriving on campus, I'd never spent a single day in Washington, DC, so there was a lot for me to check out.

In addition to the museums, the monuments, walking the National Mall regularly, and checking out the nightlife in Georgetown, the journalism program took us to many fascinating places. I've been to the Pentagon briefing room, had a small group chat with ABC News reporter Cokie Roberts, attended congressional sub-committee briefings, and the press area of the Supreme Court. Sadly, I was horribly sick the day we were supposed to go to the White House, and I still have not been there.

The experience sparked in me a sincere appreciation for the importance of journalism and the press. I saw that I could combine personal areas of strength: presentation and performance skills, journalism, and a genuine interest in finance.

As I drew closer to college graduation, in the months after my American University semester, I applied for jobs at financial institutions. Looking back, I think my belief was that I needed to prove myself in finance in order to be taken seriously in financial journalism.

Between growing up in suburban New Jersey and having an investment banker for a father, we had many connections in finance. My parents helped me get interviews at several investment firms, and I also secured some through our school career office. Overwhelmingly, the messages I received about my desire to be a financial journalist were discouraging. I felt my dreams being scoffed at, whether from a sideways glance or raised eyebrows or via direct feedback.

One of those interviews stands out more than the rest. I wore a new, navy blue suit and trekked via train and subway to a building that lived in the shadows of the Twin Towers. I also wore faux confidence announcing my arrival at the reception desk. I rode the elevator to the correct floor where I was met by my parents' friend's secretary, who took me into Mr. Not-So-Nice's office. He welcomed me with a warm handshake and, after small talk about my parents, got down to business asking me what kind of job I hoped for. I explained I wanted to learn everything there was to learn about brokering deals in investment banking and financing companies. Instead of encouraging me or asking why I thought I might be qualified, he impressed upon me the hours involved and the commitment to the work in order to be successful. The subtext in his words was, "Suzanne, why would you bother? You know you are only going to work until you meet some guy and pump out a couple of kids."

Had the discussion revolved around my skills, my courses of study, or my long-term goals, I might look back differently on that interview instead of feeling as though that man focused on my limitations rather than seeing my potential. Even if he believed the work was not the right fit for me, had he genuinely wanted to support me, he could have opened my eyes to different areas of finance or business. He could have chosen to guide me toward finding the most aligned opportunity. Instead, I left his office feeling small, defeated, and as though I was aiming too high.

Months later, through our school career office, I landed an interview for an assistant position with a stockbroker. Unlike our family friend, this guy did ask what I hoped to do. When I explained I wanted to learn as much as I could about the finance industry and investing because I ultimately wanted to be a finance journalist, he laughed in my face. Then he gruffly offered me the position at a salary so low I didn't think it would cover the cost of the almost two-hour commute from my parents' house. I politely turned it down.

Ultimately, I did what a lot of young, women college graduates of my era did: I accepted a job that was highly administrative in nature with the understanding that I wanted to move up while watching the men I graduated with accept non-administrative positions that I was every bit as qualified for.

Looking back, I lacked something important: a mentor. I needed a woman who was ahead of me on the path to show me how to fight for myself. I believe if one person told me not to take the administrative job, that I was completely capable of more, the outcome for me would have been different. This doesn't mean I would have loved working in the investment industry, or that I would have stayed in it. But I do think I would have carried more confidence with me every step I took beyond the first job.

As a coach, I get to be the mentor and cheerleader for other women, which is what I needed as a young woman. My clients move forward faster and with more confidence in whatever it is they are trying to achieve because of our work together. This is one of the privileges of my role and one of the duties. It is also the foundation of my *why*.

11

CUBICLES BE DAMNED

L ike me, many women started their careers in roles that made them feel inferior. They worked their way up the proverbial corporate ladder, perhaps getting a graduate degree along the way, and hit that Holy Grail of a six-figure paycheck they dreamed of only to question whether it made sense to work once they understood the associated costs of putting two children in daycare.

I didn't need to make the decision to leave my job. It was made for me. A company leadership change and subsequent dismissal created the opportunity for me to build my own business. At the time, my boys were one and three.

While our culture slowly changes and it's no longer odd to have men assume larger roles in childrearing, the work-life balance dynamic has not drastically shifted for most heterosexual couples. Women tend to be the caregivers and homemakers, men the breadwinners. Or more commonly, men and women both work outside the home, and women remain caregivers and homemakers, too!

I have friends who work longer hours and make more money than their husbands, yet are still in charge of all play date planning, nanny and sitter scheduling, any sick-time issues, laundry, meals, grocery shopping, most homework, housekeeper management, summer camp planning, and a large portion of extracurricular activity planning and transportation. And I wouldn't take a fifty-fifty bet on which partner is in charge of the animals!

This dynamic plays out regardless of who the primary breadwinner is, so when a woman earns less, it stands to reason that she questions her sanity for taking on both roles inside and outside the home. Layer on additional children, a child with special needs, a long commute, or job insecurity, and even women who are paid well wonder if continuing to work for someone else makes any sense at all.

As a result, there is a big shift made by women who want to provide and earn money for their professional skills outside of the corporate structure. The challenge most of these women encounter is that they've never needed to sell their work—and worth—beyond finding the job. They find themselves thrust into entrepreneurship when it was not their intention to be there.

This brings me to my *why*. I believe that women can and should be able to contribute to our households financially with the flexibility needed to care for our families at the same time. Women should be able to use their professional skills and drive, or simply their willingness to hustle, to help provide for their families. We should be able to do it around school closures, dance classes, basketball practices, and karate lessons. In a world where we can get on the phone or Internet almost anywhere, there is no reason a cubicle should be where we earn our keep. This was my *why* long before a pandemic had us all working from our homes. COVID's one saving grace is that it proved my point.

I have been in business for myself for ten years now, and, in a variety of ways, help other women gain this independence. My passion is to help women learn what they need to in order to grow healthy and strong businesses on their own time. I'm grateful every day for the opportunity to serve others in this way and humbled every time I'm told my work has been helpful.

If you are not yet in touch with your own *why*—the reason bigger than wanting to make money—I recommend taking time to think about *why* you do what you do in the context of how it supports others. Understanding your motivations and sharing them with others will serve you by connecting emotionally with your potential clients and customers and with your own desire to serve others by doing what you do.

12

RIPPLE EFFECT

E very positive thing we do affects others positively. When I've worked with entrepreneurs on understanding their *why*, I encourage them to push past the boundaries of what they can see in front of them.

Most begin focused on bringing money into their home economy to allow more freedom. Usually, this urge is tied to what they can do for their children: taking them on trips, paying for extracurricular activities, or saving for the anticipated cost of college.

These are all important desires, but as I've already shared, understanding your *why* must go deeper than the financial to keep you going during the tough times. It also must go deeper because your potential clients will not hire you simply because you want to make money.

Your *why* must start with those you serve and the effect your work will have on them. Once you understand that, you will understand what I believe is the most important part: the ripple effect. The further you realize your work can ripple, the more important your *why* can become.

I've often used the following example when teaching this to clients: let's assume for a moment that you are a massage therapist. You might like doing massage because it makes you money. To connect further to a *why*, you might decide to focus on the fact that when a woman comes to you for a massage, she leaves feeling better in her own body.

This is a start, but let's assume the massage client rarely takes time for herself and enjoying a massage is the one way she provides herself with self-care. She leaves the appointment not only feeling better in her own body, but as though she has given herself a gift. Now we've gone beyond her body to her emotional well-being.

Now let's assume that she is a working mom. She comes home every night from work exhausted, gives her children the best she has to offer them, but feels as though her cup is empty. She helps her children with their homework, and then puts them to sleep so she can get to bed as early as possible because the next day she does it all over again.

After making the time for a massage, she feels renewed. Instead of just barely getting through each evening, she takes the time to really connect with her children, to show them some extra love and attention, and to play a game with them. Her mood is lighter because she feels restored.

Her children begin to love the rare times that their mother goes for a massage because they feel the difference in her. The extra love and attention reminds them that they are the most important things in life to her.

Now remember, that in our example, you are the massage therapist. Your work created this ripple effect where a woman took care of herself and, as a result, is more available and loving to her children, building their self-worth by showing them that they are important. This is the *why* to connect to.

I use the example of a massage therapist because it is a profession with which most of my clients can relate. In my own work, I don't simply focus on the fact that I help my clients grow their businesses and make money. I recognize that, in doing so, I help them to create the freedom they need in their lives to support their families financially and in many other ways. I'm gratified and delighted that I often see them supporting, teaching, and hiring other women, too. This is the ripple effect of my work and my *why*.

You may not be a massage therapist, but if you take time to think more deeply about the ripple effect of your work, you can come up with your own example. Play it out as far as you can—well beyond what you actually see in front of you. Be creative. Your ripple effect can be anything you want it to be.

13

INTERNALIZE THIS SECTION

.

Whether you hopped onto the roller coaster of entrepreneurship intentionally, or landed in it by accident, you *will* experience the highs and lows. We all enjoy the highs: getting a new client, building to a successful launch, or receiving a testimonial that makes your heart sing. Bracing for the lows is a necessary task.

I promise you there will be moments that you consider scrapping your business. You may struggle with consistent cash flow, get overwhelmed by balancing your business and family obligations, and feel defeated by the poor response to an offering. You will want to give up at some point, despite inevitable future regret.

Your *why* is what will keep you from doing so. When you can see the bigger picture of how your work affects others positively and you realize that halting it would create a break in the chain, your perspective shifts from your momentary challenge to the greater good.

This is your opportunity to get in touch with your position in the chain and to tie it to your *why*. Consider not only what your business does for you, but also what it does for others. Think of the ripple effect your work has on the world. Examine the following:

- If you have thought about your *why* before, did you contain it to the needs of yourself and your family, or did you go beyond that?
- What is the ripple effect of your work? How far can you go with it? When you think you have gone as far as you can, take it a step further.
- Do you see how your work impacts those with whom you will never meet or interact?
- How would the disappearance of you and your work break a chain of positivity?
- If I were standing in front of you now, and asked you for your *why*, what would you share with me?

VALUES

14

VALUES

 The decisions you make are a choice of values that reflect
your life in every way.

— ALICE WATERS

Years ago, I had a boss who seemed to believe everything needed
to be done all at the same time. I joked that most people created
a priority list from the top down, but that he created his from left to
right because everything was a "top priority."

It seems an accepted truth in corporate America that mission,
vision, and values statements are necessary. The argument for them is
that they help center employees on what the company deems most
important. These statements guide employees in their daily rituals and
tasks, helping them to align everything from new product lines to
clean bathrooms. When used properly, they are exceptional tools for
everyone in the organization.

Whether working alone, or leading a company of thousands, values
inform priorities, decisions, direction, and perception. This is true,

even when we haven't taken the time to clarify and communicate them.

Each of us has a set of values that we have developed consciously and unconsciously throughout our lives. Just like the mission statements created by experts for multi-billion-dollar companies, our values inform priorities, decisions, direction, and perception. The difference is we may not be consciously aware of what our values are!

When we take time to examine our values and priorities, we reduce the stresses that come with the entrepreneurial roller coaster. Values keep us grounded and on the track most important to us. When we don't proactively understand our values, we're often presented a moment of reckoning that requires us to do so.

The reckoning might be large and highly public, as we saw in 2020 when companies shifted to support workers through a pandemic, decry racism, and alter business practices to align with stated values. The reckoning could also be quiet and private, like a mompreneur's decision to stop looking at her email or taking calls between 5 pm and 8 am in order to prioritize her family.

When I started my business, I didn't sit down and consider what my core business values were. My prevalent thought at the time was, "How the heck can I make some money?" And then it became, "How the heck can I make more money?" This is not uncommon, so if you haven't spent any time thinking about your business values before opening the first page of this chapter, don't stress about it. You are not behind! However, you'll want to consider your business values going forward.

Whatever your values are, make a commitment to them in how you run your business. Regularly check your values and how they integrate into your life and your business, especially when you're facing challenges and conflict. As you grow, be sure those who work with or for you are clear on your values and how you want your business to demonstrate them.

15

THE DINNER GUEST

In grade school, I caught the bus every morning in front of my house at a small traffic circle that seemed more like what one would find at the end of a cul-de-sac instead of a suburban neighborhood intersection. For the first few weeks of kindergarten, my mother walked me to the pick-up spot each morning to be sure I got on the bus safely. Later, she watched from the driveway, wearing her long, red bathrobe, a cup of coffee in hand.

I arrived home from school one day to the news that we were having an overnight guest. Mom and Dad's dear friend, Uncle Dennis, was coming for dinner and would stay the night. I was very excited. I'd met Uncle Dennis' family only once or twice because they lived far away, but knew his visit was special.

I enjoyed having Uncle Dennis at our house. I loved it so much that when my mother put me to bed that night, I said, "Mommy, I don't have school tomorrow."

She looked at me quizzically and asked, "Are you sure?"

"I am sure. I don't have school tomorrow," I answered, excited to see Uncle Dennis again in the morning. This is the first lie I can remember telling.

The next morning, I was shocked to find that Uncle Dennis had left the house before I woke up. My mother explained to me that he'd had an early plane to catch and departed even before my parents were up.

Minutes later, my mother received a shock when the bus rattled down the road at its usual time. She looked at me with skepticism. "Suzie! I thought you said you didn't have school today?"

I panicked. I tried to cover myself, but I'm pretty sure she saw right through my lie. It was no use. I was caught.

"Why did you lie about school today?" she asked.

I told her the truth: I wanted to see Uncle Dennis more than going to school. It was fun to have a guest at the house.

A few minutes later, mom walked me into the office at school and explained my tardiness. When I got home that day, I got in trouble for lying. It was an early and important lesson; one I clearly remember.

Honesty is one of my core values. I would rather lose the opportunity to work with someone than to suggest I can do something for her that I can't. When I don't feel a client is right for me, I let them know, and refer them to someone I believe could be a better fit. I work daily to build trust with my audience and believe the worst thing I could do is break that trust.

Too often, I've seen other business owners claim that their offer is practically guaranteed or claim ease of use for whatever is being sold. It is woefully easy to cross the line from encouraging aspiration to false claims. It is also easy to fall back on the disclaimers used in fine print at the bottom of sales pages that indicate there are no guarantees. Anyone getting good legal advice for her business will have Terms of Service posted on her website. I go a step further and ensure that anyone I work with understands that those who make lofty promises are not being truthful. It would crush me to think that anyone felt I sold her a false bill of goods. In fact, I think the best compliment I've ever gotten from a client is, "Suzanne, you're the real deal!"

C.S. Lewis said, "Integrity is doing the right thing when no one is watching." These are words to live by. When tempted to stretch the truth, even if you think you might get away with it, don't. It is far better to be known as smaller, a slower grower, or not as flashy, than to feel the shame of dishonesty, or knowing that you've taken advantage of someone's belief in you and your services.

16

BAND-AIDS AND BUBBLE GUM

I didn't know when I started out as an entrepreneur how important time freedom was to me. In 2010, I hadn't experienced much time freedom. I'd been working full-time and had two sons under the age of four. It's probably safe to say that most people in a phase of life that includes daily diaper changing are not feeling a lot of time freedom.

As Stuart and Walter got a little older, and my business got a little busier, time freedom became crucial. Play dates and sports practices were woven into the fabric of my days. Moving our family into and, a few years later, out of Vermont required considerable dedicated time. Being able to work when it made sense rather than on someone else's schedule was invaluable.

Looking at my family life today, I don't know how we would manage if I couldn't make myself available to trek our boys to those things that enrich their lives: sports, martial arts, doctors' appointments, and after school activities. I'm not so different from most parents in this regard in that my car feels most like a taxi service: required transportation that's flexible.

I've taken to working in the back seat of my car just off the side of the baseball field. I write. I organize. I know which fields or parking lots have stronger cell signals so that I can work on the web, and which require me to work without a connection. I plan my tasks accordingly. When I hop into the back seat of my Toyota Highlander, I giggle to myself that I've entered my mobile office. Typically, I switch off the radio, crack open a seltzer, place it in the cup holder and, get down to business in order to make a forty-five to ninety-minute window of time as efficient as possible.

Most days, I feel like I am holding everything together with Band-Aids and bubble gum; somehow, I make it work. Our lives will get simpler when, in another couple of years, Stuart starts driving. While that will bring new challenges and concerns, I won't need to work in the backseat of the car. For now, I'm extremely grateful that I'm the boss and I get to decide what I'm working on and when.

I do my best to remember others need time freedom too. My clients, my coaches, my team members, and my partners—virtually all of them are in a similar situation to mine. We are mothers, or caretakers, getting regularly pulled away from our work only to wish for the dedicated time to knock things off our to-do list. In keeping with time freedom as a core value of my business, I respect this need for others as much as I respect it for myself. For me, this means being clear about deadlines, consistent about communication, and providing things to my team on time.

17

SAVOR THE JOURNEY

My mother has often expressed her concern about how hard I work on my business. She asks, in a not-so-subtle way, if we really need the income from my business or if it is simply a hobby, a choice, something I could give up to simplify my life. I know these questions come from concern for and worry about me. She's a mom and desires that I live a happy, stress-free life.

There have been times when the income from my business was superfluous to our household budget. At other times, it has been an absolute necessity. Regardless, and far more importantly, the business itself is an absolute necessity to my life. It is my passion, my purpose, and my inspiration.

I love my family. I love watching my boys grow and learn. I love spending time with my husband, Kevin, either going on adventures, walking, or just watching TV. Our family is sacred to me, and, of course, Stuart and Walter are a part of me. But they will grow up and pursue their own passions. They will have careers and loves and heartbreaks. Kevin finds his own endeavors: working on our yard, golfing, researching and making fancy cocktails. I am not here to live through others' experiences. I am here to have my own.

My business makes me feel like I have a place in the world that is unique to me. It makes me excited to put my feet on the floor in the morning. Striving to increase my income from my business is a challenge I savor; one that encourages me to grow and learn every single day. It is also a vehicle through which I know I create a ripple effect. There are many activities I enjoy: puzzles, quilting, knitting, baking, playing cards, etc. But nothing fulfills me or replaces my desire to grow like my business.

I remember years ago in my virtual assistant business when I hired my first bookkeeper. I'd been in business just over a year in and she brought all of my books up-to-date. We discussed what I'd made my first year and agreed it was a respectable amount. I hired her because I was building a team, and I needed to be on top of my cash flow.

In our first call of my new business year, I shared with her that I intended to double my revenue.

"Wow," she said. "That's aggressive."

I knew my goal was a stretch, but I also knew that building a team required greater outlay of cash, so even reaching that goal would result in only a modest change in my income over the previous year. Once she understood my vision, she agreed my goal wasn't crazy.

We held quarterly review calls where we discussed my income goal and measured where I was in relation to it. Sure enough, within twelve months I had doubled my revenue. I remember the feeling of accomplishment knowing that I had achieved what I'd set out to. Part of me couldn't believe it, but I knew that my achievement had been reached due to being focused, determined, and working hard toward it every single day. Like a brilliant stroke made by a brand-new golfer, this achieved goal would be on my highlight reel.

At other times in those early years, I struggled to find happiness in the challenges that are natural in starting, running, and growing a business. The smallest setbacks felt disheartening and consequential. I cried often over my mistakes. If I invested money and didn't see an immediate return, I chastised myself for not being more capable and successful. Instead of taking responsibility for challenges in a positive way and learning from them, I beat myself up emotionally, which left me overwhelmed and exhausted.

I've worked hard to position myself so that, most of the time, I experience challenges with a much lighter heart now, occasionally even finding joy in their educational value. This transition requires me to be less attached to specific outcomes, and to forgive myself when things don't go as I would have prescribed. I learn, and apply what I've learned, making peace with myself and the process along the way.

Happiness comes in lots of different forms. Rarely does something that makes us happy come without a side of stress or challenge. I acknowledge that. The day may come when running my business no longer makes me happy. Although I struggle to imagine it, I'm open to the possibility. If it does, I'll figure out the next right step. Until then, I'm going to enjoy as much of it as possible.

18

RAINBOWS AND UNICORNS

About eleven years ago, I attended my first networking meeting. I don't remember the speaker's content, but I do remember feeling dazzled with her presentation, which focused on marketing. Based on her excellent presentation and the confidence she carried, I assumed her to be very successful. After the meeting, I investigated her website and found the offer of a digital download in exchange for my email address.

"Brilliant!" I thought. I immediately became more enamored noting this fabulous tactic for growing an email list. As a newbie to online marketing, this download was me toe-dipping in a pool of possibility. "Of course," I thought. "If you offer people something they value, they will be much more likely to give you their email address." It was as though rainbows appeared with unicorns jumping over them. What an amazing discovery!

Fast-forward six months, and it seemed everyone I knew had digital downloads on their websites. My growth in and experience of online marketing during that time was exponential. I found myself teaching others that they should create a free gift or an "irresistible free offer" in order to grow their email-marketing list. Interestingly, I told myself that I didn't know enough to charge for teaching this information; I convinced myself that I was simply offering goodwill.

No matter who you are, and how much you know about your subject matter, there will always be someone who knows more than you. As a result, it's easy to fall into the "I don't know enough to charge for my knowledge" trap.

We humans are so adaptable, that when our brains have integrated information, we forget how difficult it might have been for us to learn it in the first place. We take for granted that others know what we know when they don't. Just as there will be people who know more than you; there will always be people who know less. Sharing your knowledge with others could be a valuable game-changer in their business. Getting paid for providing that value to them is fair, appropriate, and necessary.

At some point, I recognized that giving knowledge away for free was not serving me or providing the time freedom I craved. If I wanted to stay in business, earning money was required. Amazingly, when I started charging for my hard-won information, I saw a difference in its affect. I learned that my clients were *served* by me charging them. It seems counterintuitive, doesn't it? We often think the kindest thing we can do is give our services to someone who needs them, but when I began charging for consultations, those receiving them valued their newfound knowledge more. Because they valued what I taught them and wanted a return on their investment, they got busy implementing my suggestions more quickly and, therefore, saw results more quickly.

As I transitioned further into coaching and left my virtual assistant business behind, teaching became the foundation of my business. Whether one-on-one, in a group, via Facebook Live, or otherwise, I love teaching. I love imparting upon other business owners the knowledge I've collected through my own journey. I love seeing their eyes light up with ideas, and I especially love it when I get to see them follow-through and succeed with those ideas.

If you have information that can serve someone else, in her business or her life, don't fall into the trap of believing that you don't know enough to teach it, and don't fall into the trap of giving that information away for free. You will only be hurting those you could help. When others value what you teach them by putting their money behind it, they are much more likely to receive benefit from it.

19

THE FIRST AND THE WORST

I have a distinct memory from my college admissions process. I scored a letter of recommendation from a gentleman who was a major donor to my first choice college. I'd even applied early decision, hoping it would boost my candidacy.

Between my SAT scores, private high school transcript, and that letter, I should have been able to claim a spot in their upcoming freshman class. But when I recall my interview, I know exactly why I didn't.

I was used to, and very comfortable with, being liked. Part of this probably stemmed from my genuine interest in people and desire to fit in, and part of it likely came from a natural sense of diplomacy. These attributes usually served me well, but on the occasion of my first college interview, they did not. Instead, I, the girl who so often charmed her parents' friends and had good rapport with virtually every schoolteacher and administrator I'd ever encountered, bungled my interview. Badly.

The admissions counselor asked me what I would improve or change about my high school. In retrospect, I realize she was looking for me to show some critical thinking skills. Instead of looking critically at my school, I fell right into the role I had learned so well:

pleasant young woman. I told her that the school did a wonderful job, and I wouldn't change a thing. She asked the question several times, in a few different ways. I didn't catch on.

Had I been a little savvier, and more prepared, I easily could have come up with a non-problem problem, like the ones I was later taught to provide in interviews. Answers like "my struggle is that I get too focused on my work," or "I can be a real perfectionist about getting things done on time and make mistakes because I'm tired from working late." I could have talked about a rule or two that seemed draconian—girls and women being required to wear skirts in the fall and spring trimesters and boys and men being required to wear jackets and ties all year -- or the fact that seniors didn't have a wider choice of electives. Instead, I essentially told her that everything was perfect, just hunky-dory.

I'm sure what she saw in front of her was a young, vacuous woman from an upper-middle class home with an uppity, private-school education. In that moment, I could have been any one of hundreds of girls applying to the school that year. Any originality, budding leadership, and independence was masked by my lack of interview preparation.

We all have moments in life we could have been more prepared for. This is certainly not the only interview I've flubbed, but none has stood out to me quite so starkly. The experience taught me to prepare for things that are important to me—the more important, the more preparation needed. Of all of my college interviews, that was the first and the worst. If I could turn back the clock, I would prepare for that interview with some practice ones.

Today, I know that being prepared means understanding all the steps necessary to achieve a certain outcome. It means asking questions, seeking knowledge, and making a plan, especially when I will need support. If a step seems unclear, I seek help to learn more about it ahead of time, in order to fill the void. This is what being prepared looks like, and I always want to be prepared, especially in my business.

20

BOILING POINT

W hen I was nine years old, someone asked what my father did for a living. "He sits on the couch and talks on the phone all day," I said. I was just old enough to know this was an impish response and delighted in the twitters of laughter it created.

My family had gradually been experiencing a shift in Dad's work schedule. He still worked for a company in New York City, but he worked from home more and more, atypical for the 1980s. The change came as a result of his success coupled with a desire to avoid commuting.

We all liked that Dad was around more, but our home set up wasn't conducive for a home office space. The more Dad was home, the more our family room served as his office. This created a struggle because the family room was the main thoroughfare from the garage and primary entryway to the rest of the house. My brother and I were young enough not to understand that each time we entered our house, we needed to be quiet to ensure Dad's work calls weren't interrupted. Sometimes our impassioned fighting got in the way.

About the time my father decided to work for himself, my mother began pushing for a larger home with a proper office. Dad didn't see the need. He didn't see that his work in the family room or requirements for quiet and privacy were a problem for the rest of us. He also did not want the hassle of a move. The pros and cons of a new home became a regular discussion in the household—my input typically centered around getting my own bathroom.

As most discussions between married couples do, this one simmered until it hit a boiling point. Dad dug his heels in by announcing he had no intention of moving. Mom, feeling as though she was not being heard, decided it was time she made her boundaries clear to my father. To do so, she left the house one day in the middle of the week and checked in to a hotel, leaving Dad with eleven-year-old me, my fourteen-year-old brother, our ninety-eight-year-old aunt, and two cats.

When I arrived home from school, my mom called me on my recently installed private phone line. She shared where she was and how to get in touch with her if there was an emergency. I was not to tell my dad what hotel she was in.

Two days later, she returned home. Within a few months, we moved into a new house with more space and, ultimately, built a new section of the house so Dad could have a proper office where he wouldn't be disturbed. Mom had made her boundaries clear and stuck to her guns until she made her point.

Looking back on it, I'm sure my mom did what many of us do. She allowed something that was getting under her skin to grow, rather than nipping it in the bud. When Dad first started working at home, a day or two a week in the family room probably irked her, but she had bigger issues to deal with raising our family and caring for Aunt Annie. As the number of days my dad worked from home increased and became more the rule than the exception, the challenges around him doing so grew.

We have all experienced something similar, albeit in different situations. A client begins to take advantage of us, or a team member begins to slack off. We let it pass, focusing instead on all the times they haven't. Then, because we allowed it, the behaviors happen again. Gradually, we grow so angry about the situation that it reaches a boiling point.

Every time this happens, it is because our boundaries are not clear at the start. Before I got clear on my boundaries, I used to find myself frustrated, feeling as though others were taking advantage of me. They were, but I was the one who allowed it in the first place.

I am still a work in progress on setting and holding my boundaries. However, ten years as an entrepreneur has taught me that I do need clear boundaries. Clients know that I don't work at night. They know that I don't work on the weekends unless it is my choice to do so. I communicate my expectations of them, and I respect their expectations of me. Everyone is happier that way.

In my humble opinion, my mom getting up and going to a hotel was a badass move on her part. She knew that my dad was struggling to see things from her perspective and knew he deeply loved her. She had confidence her action would help him see things from her perspective, and quickly! While I wouldn't recommend it as a go-to strategy, it served her well. I don't think she ever allowed her boundaries to be tested in the same way again. And Dad knew she meant business.

21

TELL ME WHAT YOU THINK

My junior year of college, I landed the role of student representative to the Board of Trustees. Each year, two seniors participated to provide the student perspective in relevant board discussions. This meant I got to attend a board meeting on Lake Saranac in upstate New York where the college owned a conference center.

The meeting took place in a large, rustic hall set up with auditorium style seating. The afternoon session focused on an anticipated up-leveling of the student center, the hub of all student life: mailboxes, the pub where one could get a meal outside of dining hall hours, and offices for all student clubs.

The discussion turned toward a desire to encourage student involvement in extracurricular activities. One of the adult board representatives lamented the lackadaisical attitude of many of the college's students. I raised my hand, and when called upon, shared that if the desired goal was to have more student involvement in extra-curricular activities, updating the offices provided for those activities might be an incentive. The existing space provided was tired, dingy, and inhospitable. In other words, not a place I wanted to spend much time. My comments sent the room aflutter.

Dinner that evening was a group event at which the two student board reps were expected to sit apart from one another in order to mingle with the regular board members and their spouses. I sat next to a gentleman whose son I knew from campus. We exchanged pleasantries about college life, my experience of his son, and his own experience of the school many years before. Naturally, there were also discussions about the day's topics.

At one point, my dining companion looked at me and said, "Well, you're blunt. Tell me what you think."

His statement took me aback. No one had ever asked for my opinion like that and being described as blunt shocked me. Without thinking, I responded wryly, "I believe you mean direct, don't you?" Ever since, I have giggled to myself about proving his point while suggesting otherwise. He took my response with good humor, thank goodness.

No one, before or since, has ever described me as blunt, at least not to my face. I do, however, almost always have an opinion. I believe it is healthy to have opinions and to express them. It is also healthy to listen to others' opinions and consider how and why they differ from your own before judging them.

So many of us hold back from expressing our opinions because we're concerned they might be considered wrong or invalid. Building confidence in sharing your thoughts is important to learning, growing, and serving others. There are ways and times to share your ideas, and learning these skills is vital. Equally important is learning that your opinion matters, that others aren't all-knowing, and sharing your opinion enriches those around you.

Thought leadership, by definition, is having and sharing an opinion that is not already expressed by others. Undoubtedly, your opinion may ruffle some feathers, as anything novel does. If it is your goal to be considered a thought leader, get bolder in sharing your opinions. Build confidence, and resilience. You will need all of that, and more.

22

BAKED POTATOES

I dislike baked potatoes with a burning hot passion. Somewhat ironically when I actually eat one, I sometimes enjoy them. It's what potatoes represent to me that displeases me.

Between my freshman and junior years of high school, a few things converged. My brother moved out of the house to attend boarding school and later college; my parents were invited to and attended many fundraisers both locally and in New York City; and I was old enough to spend evenings alone at home. As a generally responsible kid, my parents didn't worry about leaving me on those nights they had other obligations. I got my schoolwork done, got off the phone at a reasonable hour, and wasn't the type to hold a party in their absence. I was also very content alone.

Living in New Jersey meant that I was unable to get a driver's license until I was seventeen, so I didn't have one until just before the start of my senior year. This meant that when Mom and Dad left home at 4:30 p.m. for a 6 p.m. fundraiser in the city, one challenge remained: what would Mom feed me for dinner? (Remember, this all occurred before the invention of DoorDash and UberEats.) We did not live within walking distance of town, and takeout choices in suburban New Jersey were not what they are today.

This left my mother with a simple but elegant solution: a baked potato. I vividly remember the notes I'd find after play rehearsal or cheerleading practice:

Dear Suzie,

Dad and I are in New York at XYZ fundraiser and will be home late. There is a baked potato in the oven for you.

Love,
Mom XOXO

One could argue that I felt abandoned and that the baked potato became a symbol of the abandonment. I think the truth is that I just got really sick of them. When I reminisce, I recall how grand it felt to see my parents dressed up, usually in black tie, for events they attended. My mother had a collection of beautiful gowns and I'd love to see what she wore each time and see her sashay out the door wearing her fur coat.

Of course, my parents didn't just attend fancy events, they also volunteered. Starting when I was five, I remember my mom telling me she would be at the Friends of the Library meeting or my dad saying he would be at the Morris Museum board meeting. For a number of years, my mother pulled together the Friends of the Library newsletter. I'd find her at the bottom of our basement stairs, hunched over a desk and an electric typewriter, typing up articles or announcements. She'd manually lay out her typed articles on an 8½ x 11 piece of paper, frustrated when she was one line too long.

In addition to the museum, Dad was a trustee of his college and my brother's private school. He'd often head out for the evening or away for the weekend to upstate New York to attend various meetings.

Giving back to our community was an important value in our family, one that my parents passed down and that has continued to be my norm. Over the years, I've been on college and graduate school fundraiser committees, hospital fundraiser committees, local theater fundraiser committees, and the parent associations of my children's schools, etc. When asked, one can usually get me to contribute in some way to a cause, and I've been willing to take on leadership roles when I've seen how I could serve. Giving and volunteering are important to me, and are both something I feel is important to model for my children, as my parents did for me.

What getting involved taught me was exactly how important it is. The smaller your community is, the more important. When we lived in Vermont in a town of three to four thousand people, more volunteer opportunities existed than people to fill them. When I assumed a leadership role with the school parents' association (PTO), just how desperately we needed volunteers became crystal clear. The elementary and middle school served approximately 300 students, yet only five to six mothers consistently showed up to PTO meetings. Another five or six occasionally volunteered their time.

This meant in order to provide any event to the student community, the very few worked like crazy. It was exhausting and frustrating. While there were parents who thanked us for our hard work, there were some who shared how they thought we could have run the events better. Even more exhausting were the excuses from those who couldn't be bothered to volunteer.

One of the women who ran our PTO for several years was most creative and gave more time than any other volunteer—and did so between phone calls to her son's surgical teams. She never made excuses for what she couldn't do; instead, she used whatever time she had to create a positive experience for all the kids in our community.

I think of her when I get an email asking for someone to take a shift at our school book fair, or to sell bracelets for upcoming school events. My first reaction every single time is, "I can't possibly fit that in on top of everything else." Then I stop and remember what a difference it makes to volunteer even just one or two hours. Our tiny band of mothers appreciated any help we received. What I would have given for a few more people to take a two-hour shift, and what a difference it would have made to those of us who otherwise needed to fill it.

We are all tired. We are all overworked. Few of us have the luxury of single breadwinner households that create opportunity for the other spouse to give back more. It is always easier to stay home in the evening than it is to get out to a meeting after a family dinner. However, in doing so, we are often richly rewarded. We meet the those who are truly willing to give of themselves, and we go to bed at night knowing we have made a difference.

And good news: your kids probably already know how to get food delivered right through their smart phones. No baked potatoes necessary!

23

INTERNALIZE THIS SECTION

I n the first few years of The Implementation Station, I felt torn in many directions. My children were younger and needed consider-able energy. As a result, my marriage struggled for attention. I traded my work time for money and tried to keep my head above water to help pay necessary bills. Creating a vision statement for my business or aligning my business decisions to my values was not on my radar. Since then, and over time, I've seen how values unconsciously created an impact—thankfully, mostly good.

I have become more conscious of my core values and ensure they are exemplified in my business. If you haven't taken the opportunity to review your values and consider their influence, you'll want to do that sooner than later. Here are some areas to consider:

- In our marketing, we tend to focus on the promised outcomes we provide to potential clients. It is human for our prospects to want these outcomes to be easy and to come without stress. What do you promise to your clients and how do you communicate that promise? Is your promise in line with your core values?
- Are your values around your loved ones and where they fit

into your life honored by the boundaries you've created for yourself related to your business? Do you need to examine your time boundaries further?

- Do you enjoy all the elements of your work? If you do not, are there ways you could give that work to others in order to create more pleasure from your business?
- Are you valuing your knowledge and teaching others to value what you provide to them?
- Are you prepared to accept opportunities that come your way? How could you be more prepared to say yes to things that align with your vision?
- What are you tolerating that is holding you or your business back? How can you shift it to be more aligned with your desired outcomes?
- Are you fully voicing your perspective and opinions? Do you hold back concerned that they won't be in alignment with a partner, client, colleague or others in your industry?
- Are you giving to your community in a way that aligns with your beliefs and your position? If not, what shift is needed for alignment?

MINDSET

24

MINDSET

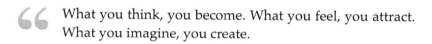 What you think, you become. What you feel, you attract.
What you imagine, you create.

— BUDDHA

It has taken me years to feel I have any understanding of the concept of mindset. I used to think it was simply how we thought about things. Now I know mindset means a whole lot more. Mindset is a combination of thoughts, feelings, responses, and attitudes that affect how we interact consciously and subconsciously with everything and everyone around us. Even though my mindset has evolved considerably, I still feel like I learn about it every day.

Growing my mindset has been integral to my personal and business growth. While many who've known me for years might not be aware of the changes, I am keenly aware of my internal shifts, and all for the better.

25

THE DEVILS

I've heard it said that the ability for a business to grow is only as great as its owner's capacity to grow. My growth has come in fits and starts, as has the growth of my business. What I know for sure—thank you, Oprah—is that every time I commit to grow in a certain area, or to develop myself, I see positive things come from that commitment in my business.

For example, when I started my virtual assistant business, I invested in learning all about online systems. At that time, I took on the challenge, saw what people needed, and learned about the topic. It didn't take long before clients came to me for my expertise and referred their friends. My willingness to grow my skill set directly impacted my ability to serve, and therefore, grew my client base.

Later, I learned to value my own services. In order to grow to the next level, I wanted to increase my prices, but first I had to truly believe that what I offered was worthy of a larger investment. This belief required learning more about my marketplace and pricing models. I dug in, researched how other virtual assistant teams were run, and solicited advice from people with more experience than me. Before long, I raised my prices, passed work to team members, and watched our client base expand again.

You may have heard the truism "new level, new devil," which means that no sooner have we solved a problem or crossed a benchmark than a new challenge presents itself. I remember wishing for team members to help me with all the work we had in order to allow my company, The Implementation Station, to grow. Once I had these employees, I had a new learning curve: managing them without being a bottleneck. We can see each new challenge as a cross we must bear, or we can see each as an opportunity for growth.

A few years ago, after being a member of my team for about six years, Bernadette and I connected on a call. I hadn't brought on new virtual assistant clients because I was more focused on my coaching business. Bern was responsible for servicing one client we'd been supporting since the days before I had her.

"I just can't do it anymore, Suzanne." She said, "They are going in a new direction, and I feel I need to focus in other areas that bring in more money." I'd suspected for a while that Bern maintained this client more out of loyalty to me than anything.

Despite knowing this, my first reaction to her news was to panic. The client provided my business with a recurring source of monthly income, which was more than could be said for my coaching business. Immediately, my wheels started turning and fixated on the hassle of finding a replacement. Then I stopped myself, realizing the gift in Bernadette's decision. We'd kept this client out of a sense of loyalty even though neither of us felt invested in the work we provided to them. The client deserved to find a support team that would be emotionally invested in their success. In releasing them, we created space and energy for new and better opportunities.

When we learn to focus on the opportunity for growth, stress and strain that we experience eases with each step forward. This mindset allows us to accept our challenges and failures. Both will occur.

Throughout my years in business, expanding my growth mindset has taught me to dig deeper into why I think the things I do. I've learned to focus on where my thoughts originate. This shift led to very large, positive changes in my outlook and business. As always though, with new learning comes new challenges: new level, new devil.

26

SOUNDS CRAZY, RIGHT?

"Success in business is twenty percent marketing, knowledge, timing, and opportunity and eighty percent mindset," my mentor said from the stage in front of me. What? I'd had a couple of glasses of wine with dinner, so I thought perhaps I'd misheard. She followed it with, "Sounds crazy, right?"

I had heard her correctly.

The three-day conference I attended focused primarily on marketing and getting clients, but one of the evenings was set aside for our mentor to teach a little bit about mindset and how we have control over our own thoughts. I'd heard about the Law of Attraction—after all, *The Secret* had already been produced and I watched Oprah. But I had no real understanding of the concepts and how they work in our lives.

My mentor dove deep into the differences between our conscious thoughts and our unconscious thoughts. We learned that no matter how much we think our actions are dictated by our conscious thoughts, it is the unconscious ones that guide us and impact our behaviors. My mind was blown. The experience kick-started a desire to learn more about my mindset and how to leverage it for success.

In the years since, I have learned so much about mantras,

Emotional Freedom Technique, Psych K®, and other ways of accessing my subconscious. I've begun to understand how our brains are wired, yet I feel as though I have only seen the tippety-top of an enormous iceberg. As I sit in front of my computer and tap out this chapter, I have moments of feeling like a fraud. I wonder if I don't know enough to include a chapter in this book on mindset. I also know if I don't tackle the importance of mindset for business, I will leave a glaring hole.

If you haven't been introduced to mindset study, a great place to start is by learning a few things about the human brain. Our brains process between six and sixty thousand thoughts per day—which helps me understand why I am so darn tired every evening! Can you relate?

Of these thoughts, eighty percent are negative. Eighty percent! Our brains are wired to think negative, self-preserving thoughts from the caveman days when we had to be on the lookout for things like saber-toothed tigers. Thousands of years ago, these negative thoughts kept us safe. The brain hasn't caught on to the fact that we don't experience the same level of physical danger as we did back then. Today, the brain, or ego, keeps us so safe that we don't expose ourselves to challenges well within our grasp.

Our brains are hard-wired to protect us. They receive triggers from other systems in our body, like the hormone levels that shift when we are about to step on stage to speak. The triggers turn into protective thoughts, and those thoughts turn into what we perceive as feelings, like fear; hence the reason so many people are filled with fear at the idea of making presentations. Understanding the brain's process is the first step to breaking it down and unraveling how our conscious thoughts impact our actions.

Entrepreneurs constantly put themselves in a position to feel fear. Whether presenting on stage, writing a book, creating a new company, course, product, service, or marketing campaign, we consistently push boundaries that send those negative thought triggers to our brain. Because of this, it is imperative for us to learn to counterbalance them —and one of the major reasons we need our tribe of roller coaster riders around us. We all experience similar challenges—most of which are self-inflicted.

That's also the reason our success is based eighty percent on our mindset. The strength of our ability to move through the negative thoughts directly impacts everything we do to create, build, and sustain our businesses.

27

RADIO STATIONS

When I was introduced to the concept of energy vibration and its relationship to the law of attraction, my thought was, "Now this is some really whack-a-doodle stuff!" If you respond negatively to what I share here, I fully and completely accept where you are coming from, and I don't blame you one bit if you think I'm a little nuts. (You would be in good company!)

That said, the longer I have lived since first hearing of these concepts, the more I see them at work and I'm open to the possibility that there is truth within them. I share without hesitation that I do not consider myself an expert in this arena but feel as though I would be missing an opportunity if I didn't at least introduce these concepts to you.

A basic definition of Law of Attraction is the ability to attract into our lives whatever we focus on. The tricky part to understand is that the Law works whether we are focused on the positive or the negative.

For example, sometimes, you'll wake up feeling poorly and have the premonition that a crappy day awaits. Suddenly, the coffee machine doesn't work, the kids are screaming, and the car stalls out. Or perhaps you feel frustration trying to complete a project. There it is: the crappy day you knew you were going to have.

Conversely, those days you wake up to sunshine streaming through your window and you just know it is going to be a great day. You don't let little things bother you because you feel you had such a great night's sleep. It's okay that you needed to run out for a coffee because your coffee maker was on the fritz again, and you feel relieved that the kids made their way onto the bus so you could tackle your big project. There it is: the beautiful day you anticipated.

These are simplified examples, but in each scenario, your belief, or your thought, about the type of day you expected created that type of day. The good news is we have the power to change our thoughts and, in doing so, create better days. The bad news is that we are pre-programmed to have negative thoughts. We have the opportunity to re-program them, but it requires concentrated effort.

So how do we shift these negative thoughts into positive ones? Before I get to that, I want to share how thoughts, feelings, or emotions feed off of each other within us and how they work together to create either positive or negative outcomes.

For example, yesterday I felt stressed about the amount of work I had to complete. As I thought about the work and the items on my to-do list, my stress levels rose. When my dog interrupted me needing to go out, my thought was, "I have too much to do to take you out again." These thoughts created feelings of frustration, additional stress, and even a twinge of anger.

On other days, when I could use a break and Lily jumps off of her chair and looks to me for an outing, I feel grateful for her for making me get up and move. Her tail wag and attention remind me how lucky I am to have her in my life. And on days when it's simply gorgeous outdoors, I feel especially grateful for her example and the opportunity to get outdoors in the middle of the day.

How we are feeling, affects the thoughts we have, and the thoughts we have affects how we are feeling. It's a great big circle. The tricky part is that our feelings have frequencies just like radio stations. Those frequencies affect our ability to attract what we want. When feelings are positive, they are at a higher frequency than when feelings are bad. Higher frequency feelings allow us to attract the good, but lower frequency feelings repel.

If you are new to this concept of the Law of Attraction, you may wonder why the heck it's important enough to include it in this book. Here's the reason: if you are about to offer something amazing to your potential clients and customers, but you feel worried or insecure about doing so, you will be in a state of non-attraction. Worry and insecurity are vibrations that repel rather than attract. To attract a positive response, you want to be in an attracting, or positive, emotional state. The good news is, just like a radio station, you can, with practice, easily turn the dial and quickly shift your emotional state with the knowledge of where you want to go.

Esther and Jerry Hicks of Abraham-Hicks Publications created a wonderful Emotional Guidance Scale if you'd like to study this further, but I'll summarize it here: higher vibration emotions like joy, gratitude, and love attract. Lower vibration emotions like hatred and anger repel. These are the extremes. Then there are feelings that sit in the middle of the scale, such as feeling content. Contentment will attract, but not as much as joy or love. Boredom repels, but it doesn't repel as much as fear or grief.

In every moment of our lives, we are either in an emotional state that attracts or repels. We also have positive or negative thoughts. Our emotional state and thoughts all work in concert to create our experience.

You might ask, "Does this mean I'm supposed to always be in a state of joy? Is there something wrong with me if I'm not?" No. No human will ever consistently be in any one state. We move through different thoughts and emotions all the time. What I have personally found though is the more I find myself in positive, attracting emotions, the more I attract what I want into my life. Therefore, the easier it is to stay in the high vibration emotions.

And it makes perfect sense! Think about it this way: we have all known people who regularly have something negative to say. Perhaps they habitually blame outside forces for their reduced fortunes—her boss was a no-good jerk, which is why she quit and now makes less money; her husband came home late every night and that's why she left him; or the cleaning lady never cleans the windows properly.

These are people we don't tend to want to hang around. We often find ourselves looking for excuses as to why we might not be able to get together with them or attend a gathering they are organizing. They repel us.

Conversely, we all know people who seem to find a positive spin on anything that goes on around them. They talk about how the rain will help the flowers grow or avoid a drought. They consistently have something new and fun they want to tell us about. They love their work and how it impacts people. They are just grateful that the car accident wasn't worse.

These people attract us. We like to be with them because they like life. When they invite us to join them on an adventure we want to go because we usually have a great time with them. We'll cancel another obligation to go to their party because their friends are upbeat and fun, too. We are attracted to them and that which surrounds them.

The knowledge of this emotional scale has greatly impacted both my work and personal life. It's not that I don't occasionally find myself in a repelling state. I've learned that repelling state is not the place I want to stay and know the faster I shift the radio station, the better off I'll be.

There are two major take-aways here: how to change your thoughts, and how to change your emotions. Both start with recognizing the state you are currently in and knowing when you want to change it.

There are many ways to shift your thoughts. I'll share two that help me.

The first tool that serves me is mantras. When I find myself thinking something negative, I will turn the thought around into something positive. For example, I turn, "I hate paying bills" into "I'm grateful to pay those who serve me and my family" or "What the heck am I going to feed my kids tonight?" to "I'm lucky for a wide variety of choices I have for feeding my family." When I repeat these mantras, I feel a shift in my body. The tension releases, my shoulders drop, my breathing deepens, and I am immediately reminded that I want my thoughts to continue to be positive.

The second way I shift my thoughts is meditation. I'm not a consistent meditator, but when my thoughts feel overwhelming, meditation helps me considerably. I find a quiet place and simply breathe in and out, focusing on my breath. Occasionally, I use the Insight Timer app on my phone to help focus my meditation on something specific. I find that, even in as little as five minutes, meditation releases tension in my body and reminds me that I want my conscious thoughts to be positive.

Shifting emotions can be different for everyone, but there are some commonalities. Doing something you love can immediately create happiness. If you like to go for a walk, do it. If playing with your dog brings you joy, take time out to do so. If singing show tunes in the shower is your thing, get to it!

Knowing what makes you happier, more positive, and joyful is a gift. If you don't know what it is as you read this, find out! And if you do know those actions that lift you up, find a way to do more of them. Doing so will raise your vibration frequency, set your station to the right tunes, and enable you to attract more of what you want into both your business and your life.

28

THREE HUNDRED DOLLARS

My hands were shaking as I pulled out my credit card to purchase a program to help me attract more clients and make more money. Three monthly payments of ninety-nine dollars—three hundred dollars—though it could have been thirty thousand for the heaviness I felt in the pit of my stomach. My ego fought my heart about investing that much money, but I knew I needed the help. If this woman could solve my problems, I wanted what she was selling.

I vividly remember the first time I made any investment in coaching support for my business. On one hand, it seemed illogical to me that I would need it—I had an MBA in marketing and entrepreneurship after all. On the other hand, I was tired of struggling.

Every year for five years, I attended a Mindset Retreat. The first year, when the discussion of money came up, I watched with interest as the retreat leader laid out her case showing how many of us have been programmed to believe that wealthy people are horrible people and generally unpleasant to be around. She taught us that, at best, they were often depicted as buffoons who didn't see what was going on around them. Conversely, she showed us that people without money were portrayed as genuine and caring. They were usually the heroes of any story. Great examples of these depictions are Goldie Hawn and

Kurt Russell's characters in the movie *Overboard* in which Goldie plays an extremely wealthy, unpleasant heiress and Kurt plays a genuine but poor widowed father.

I didn't believe I had mindset issues around money. I thought that because I knew plenty of wealthy people and did not look negatively upon them the money mindset discussion didn't apply to me. I sat politely in the audience that first year and mentally checked the box on money mindset issues, thinking I was ready to move on to the next category. If you haven't caught on yet, I was wrong!

As I attended that retreat in subsequent years, I gradually unveiled the layers of my money story. I watched friends invest more readily in their businesses and make consistent progress while holding myself back from doing both. During the process of growing, I learned I have a deep need for financial security.

You might think, "Who doesn't?" And, of course, you would be right. We all need financial security. But unlike many, I've never had to live without a solid safety net. Starting my own business, I entered a time where my net felt less secure. Fear of this unknown state gripped me.

By all external measures, my family had everything we needed, and did not need to worry, but I struggled. It held me back from making investments in both my business and my personal life.

Looking back, I wish that my husband and I had done more traveling before we had children. I also wish we'd taken more time for the two of us, away from our kids for occasional weekends when our children were younger. We could have done more of this, but I felt we shouldn't spend the money. I felt that we had to prepare for the worst and should be saving for a rainy day.

This belief came from the values I was taught about saving from a very young age. I can remember my father saying, "Everything I do, I do for you kids." My grandfather dropped dead of a heart attack at age forty-five, and my father lived believing he would too. This led him to focus on and plan for an early death for himself. Countless times, he told me of life insurance policies, trusts, and living wills he had made because, "You know, Suzie, every year past the age of forty-five is a gift for me. I don't expect it."

He also taught me about credit cards and investing from a young age. He spoke about having a balance on a credit card like it was the worst thing that could happen to a person. For many years, I believed it was. Now, while still extremely mindful about credit card debt, I know it can be a useful tool for growth.

What I have come to understand is that investing in my business pushes me, and it, forward. Without those investments, I stagnate. I hoped that things would get better but struggled at times to focus on what needed to grow. Investment was like rocket fuel for me. When I saw an area where I needed support and I invested in getting help, I became more diligent about my growth.

Consider this book for a moment. Almost five years ago, I began writing a business book with the intention to publish it in early 2015. That book still exists within my computer files. No one has seen it, and I don't think I will ever publish it. Had I done so back then, it would have represented where I was in my business, and it likely would have supported my future growth. At the time, I tried to do everything on a shoestring budget. That showed in my approach to the book, and my commitment to have it published.

Having spent the past five years chiding myself about finishing it and "getting it out there," I decided in 2020 that it was the time for me to publish. I pulled up the files and began to read through them. In the process, I realized how much I've matured, personally and as a business owner.

That book was no longer the one I needed to send out into the world. I knew it, and when I decided what I needed to write, I got busy finding someone to support me with all that would be required to bring it to completion. It was scary for me to invest in this book. My desire to do it on a shoestring budget was still pretty fierce. Yet I made the more mature choice to get the right help, to publish a quality book I would be proud of.

I put money behind my goal. As a result, I created a commitment to myself and to a publisher that this book would be written. I have a plan, deadlines, and a firm commitment. This is how money works in business. It creates energy around what needs to be done. When you realize what your goals are, put your money behind them and watch your business grow.

While I am still, and expect I always will be, careful with money, I am much better today about seeing the big picture of my financial decisions. I put finances in the context of our overall lives and evaluate spending and investment differently. As a result, I've grown, and my business has grown. When I think back to when I spent that three hundred dollars, I feel my shaking hands, and the nervousness sprinting through my body, I am grateful for the lessons and growth that came with it. They are unquantifiable but are easily worth more to me today than three hundred dollars.

29

MONDAY MORNING REVEAL

Anyone who has grown up in the era of Oprah is aware of gratitude journals. That doesn't mean we've been wise enough to keep them. I have tried at times, but I'm nothing if not inconsistent, so you can imagine how well I've done!

As a student of mindset, I work to fully understand the connection between gratitude, our beliefs, and happiness. Synthesizing these together will likely be a lifelong pursuit. After all, having a positive mindset is not a static state of being. It is a practice. I equate it with building and maintaining a healthy muscle rather than with the flipping of a light switch. We don't suddenly understand positive mindset and say to ourselves, "Cool. I'm going to do that." It takes integration in every aspect of our lives.

When I first learned of gratitude journals, I thought they were just a way for us to begin or end the day on a positive note—a way to make us feel better about things. Although this simple way of viewing keeping a gratitude journal is correct, the truth is their power is much greater than it seems. The connection between gratitude and our ability to achieve more is undeniable. When we feel genuine gratitude and focus on it, we stop looking for what is wrong and begin to see only what is right and positive. In doing so, we raise our vibration, making us able to attract more of what we want.

Years ago, one of my clients played a key role in teaching me this lesson. About two years into my virtual assistant business, I supported a coach—we'll call her Cathy—through the launch of her new program. We planned for weeks, executed flawlessly, and anticipated amazing results. Cathy had previously launched other programs and often sold fifteen to twenty women into each. The cart closed on Sunday night at midnight.

Monday morning, I tingled with excitement just thinking about logging into Cathy's system to see how many sales came in Sunday evening. Having supported her throughout the development and sales process, I was hooked on the adrenaline. When my computer screen updated to reveal the answer, my heart sank. Only five women stepped up and joined her program.

Anticipating a call with Cathy later that morning, I prepared myself to be a supportive team member. When a friend needs a shoulder to cry on, I get my shoulder ready. When we connected, Cathy was all business: on-boarding details, next steps, and follow-ups on other revenue streams. I expressed my concern and frustration about the lack of sales, and she surprised me by seeming extremely happy with her results. "The women who were meant to step forward did," she said. "Everything happens exactly the way it is supposed to."

I wondered if she was putting on a brave face for her team—if she had actually spent part of the morning crying and just didn't want her team to know. I knew that if roles were reversed, that's what I would have done.

In retrospect, I believe she spoke her truth. She was further down the path from me in understanding gratitude and its connection to achieving more. If she felt any angst, it came and went quickly, and she chose to focus her mind on what was good: the five amazing women who had stepped forward into her program. She provided a great lesson for me.

I do my best imperfectly to look for the good in any situation. Sometimes it is easy to find. Other times I need to work harder, but I can always find something good. I have developed my mindset to the point where I can find things to be grateful about no matter what my situation. For example, I am writing this at the end of 2020 when the world is gripped by COVID-19.

I feel great gratitude for:

- My health and that of my family;
- Our home, which is cozy, warm, and large enough that my family of four can be here comfortably day-in and day-out;
- The knowledge that we, and our children, will not go hungry;
- The ability to sit in my home office and do my work;
- The fact that I don't have to wear a mask all day;
- The two days of school per week that my children attend in person;
- Our dog, who loves to snuggle with me;
- The convenience of being able to order a lot of stuff through Amazon; and
- The fact that I can now get the brand of toilet paper I like (little things matter!).

I do not feel gratitude for COVID itself. Yet, I can list some positive things that have come from it:

- More family time;
- The fact that most of the time I really don't need to worry about what to wear;
- Less running around and driving my kids all over the place;
- The innovation by companies who have created vaccines at lightning speed; and
- The likelihood that many people will commute less in the future.

Next-level learning is to be grateful for challenging experiences. I don't think I will ever get to the point where I will see COVID as a good thing, but I can look back at other experiences with appreciation for how they helped me grow. For example, you've already read about the challenges I've faced like the banker who made me feel small or absolute failure of a tele-class I held. While I would not choose these experiences again, I am grateful for what I learned. Other challenges you'll read about later have shown me the strength in my marriage. Kevin and I are blessed with the knowledge that things might get pretty darn bad, but neither of us is walking away because of it.

Interestingly, gratitude and forgiveness are tied together more than most people realize. There's a famous quote from Oprah, "True forgiveness is when you can say, 'Thank you for that experience.'" A word of caution: beginners can't just jump into this practice. For a long time, I thought this concept was simply nuts! Now I find it to be true.

There are many stories in this book based on unpleasant experiences, such as the client who stiffed me, the virtual assistant team members who came and went quickly, or our Vermont departure. I see now that I've grown through every single one of them, and I can look back and feel gratitude because I love the life I have right now.

The teachers of those lessons play a role in the person I am today. And I like the person I am today. So why shouldn't I feel a sense of gratitude toward them instead of the anger I may have felt at the time. It is likely they think much less of our experiences together. If they do think of them, I hope they can see the good and the bad in them as I do. Perhaps they don't think of those moments at all, or perhaps they carry guilt about them. This is none of my business. What is my business is keeping my energy high, serving those I am able to serve, and continuing to learn and grow.

I do this by continuing to focus on gratitude, albeit not in a journal.

30

AMAZON PACKAGES

No matter who you are or how in love with your spouse you are, marriage can be challenging under the best of circumstances. Pile on some kids, parents with health issues, job losses, and physical separation—marriage is not for the faint of heart.

Mine has experienced all of the above and more. I'm grateful that it is in its seventeenth year and that my husband and I are still pretty happy each day to wake up next to one another. Like any relationship, ours has had ups and downs. Understanding my own mindset has been extremely helpful to me in keeping our marriage healthy and one I want to be in.

In any relationship, the closer we get, and the longer we are together, the easier it is to make assumptions about what the other person is thinking or feeling. Over time, those assumptions can multiply and take on a life of their own. We assume that we know others' thoughts based on previous responses. The reality is we never know what someone else is thinking or feeling unless we ask them.

A number of years ago, I wanted to make a sizable investment in my business. It was the kind I would not make without discussing it with my spouse. In truth, I had wanted to make this specific investment for several years but, as I've already shared, I struggled with making business investments.

For a few years, instead of speaking to my husband about it, I made the assumption that he would not support me in making the investment, which was unfair. I believed just bringing up the idea would cause a fight. Given that my belief was we would fight, I'm sure we would have. At the time, if Kevin had shown any hesitation, my response would have been to assume he didn't want me to make the investment. Of course, I would have allowed myself also to create the story that he didn't believe in me.

However, after several years of working on and understanding my mindset, I examined the scenario further. I remembered that I tend to make decisions very quickly and that Kevin needs time to contemplate them. Rather than seeing that as a flaw in him, I considered how this personality trait often serves us very well.

I accepted that we would not have one simple conversation ending with, "Sure, honey. Go spend that ten thousand dollars." I knew that he would need to digest my request. In accepting all this, I realized that my desire for an immediate *yes* was just that, a desire, not a necessity. I also realized that his need to process the request didn't stem from a lack of trust or support. It was simply his process.

We had the conversation. He processed. He supported me, just as I expected he would.

The lesson of this experience has been invaluable to me in my marriage. It took me years to learn, but now that I know it, it consistently serves me well. "Have faith," I tell myself when other situations come up that we don't see eye to eye on. This doesn't mean we don't have our fair share of arguments. We do. We are both strong-willed people. But in the moments after a blow up, when my thinking brain is back in my head, I go back to what I believe to be true about him, "He loves you. He wants to do the right thing just as much as you do. He needs time to process your perspective on this."

The shift from having a fight to not having a fight regarding the investment had almost nothing to do with Kevin. It was almost entirely about the way I approached the situation. My expectation and my acceptance that his immediate response might not be a gleeful, "Go for it!" was a game-changer. I set my expectation around the ultimate outcome—which of course was most important to me. As a result, I got both what I expected and what I wanted—his loving support.

Another example of shifting my mindset about our relationship related to the packages that regularly arrived on our doorstep. I'm sure I'm not the only one who is amazed at the volume of packages arriving at her home. These days, we all enjoy the convenience of discovering a household or personal need, then click, click, clicking, and having our need fulfilled within a day or two.

Kevin gets excited about even the smallest of purchases. As a result, whether returning home from his pre-pandemic commute, or coming downstairs from his home office (also known as our bedroom) at the end of the day, he delights in opening packages as soon as possible. It is not uncommon for this opening to happen just as I am putting dinner on the table, a time when I'd really appreciate the packaging and its refuse not entering the kitchen. It enters anyway!

In the past, his actions would really get under my skin. I found it especially tiresome because Kevin's habit is to open the item, and then move immediately into fix-it mode. When roles are reversed, I will delay the opening of a package until it is a "good time" for me to deal with its anticipated contents and packaging.

New wrapping paper ordered through the school fundraiser might wait in its box for a day or two before being opened and placed in our wrapping paper holder in the basement. A new article of clothing I've purchased might wait on my desk in its package until I am ready to try it on. If I know it fits, it might wait weeks until the day I am ready to wear it. New clothes for our boys will wait until I'm ready to clip the tags and put them all in the laundry.

When I move forward with the opening, I deal immediately with the refuse. Otherwise, I end up lamenting its existence. Kevin can go days without seeming bothered by packaging on the kitchen counter or dining room table.

For years, him leaving package waste drove me nuts. I steamed internally, creating a belief in my head that his leaving of refuse was a reflection of his respect level for me. I would stare at the packaging for days waiting for him to come along and toss it or break it down for recycling. I found myself internally adamant that I would not clean up his messes. Of course, each passing day my frustration grew.

I believe Kevin was as clueless to my feelings as he currently is to the solution. One day, as I looked at the latest cardboard box left on the kitchen island, I thought, "Why does he leave this stuff like this? How can he not know it drives me nuts?"

This time, a different answer came to me. "This has absolutely nothing to do with you, Suzanne. He is excited to see the packages when he gets home and loves to open them right away. It's nice to come home after a long day of work to a package."

With this realization, I dug further, "You know, Suz, you get the freedom to manage your days the way you want to. He only has a few hours a day after work that he's not in meetings or working on what needs to be provided at the next meeting. Lighten up! Throw the packaging away yourself. He does a lot for you!"

So now, when a package comes to the house, and the refuse is left on the kitchen island, I look at it and usually throw it away pretty quickly myself. I don't lament it; I don't get frustrated. I remember that Kevin does a lot for me and I'm really grateful for the time freedom I have that allows me to take care of our boys and still run my business.

This feels a lot better! And whether Kevin realizes it or not, it's a small way that the energy in our house has improved from all the positive mindset work I do and will continue to do.

How does this relate to your business, your partner, your supporters? The small niggles you deal with daily that become big things in your head when they really aren't. This is about understanding your thoughts and how they influence you, positively or negatively. It's about developing a mindset muscle to create the positive thought patterns in your head which you want there, rather than the negative ones that keep you in a state where you repel what you want: success, happiness, flow.

I am far from an expert at mindset work. I feel more like a baby constantly learning new aspects, but I feel compelled to share what I've learned because of how even my beginner's knowledge positively impacted my business and daily life.

31

THAT VOICE

M y MBA program prided itself on making us work in groups. The leadership of the program surmised that whether we were departing to build our own businesses or matriculating into larger companies we would spend much of our future careers working collaboratively. As a result, all our projects seemed group based.

During my second year of the program, I participated in a project that worked on a competitive analysis of an online toy company. It was a semester long endeavor, with a team of four people, so we got to know our teammates pretty well.

Toward the end of the semester, we met late in the day and joked about heading to the campus pub immediately afterward. I don't remember the context of our conversation, but I vividly recall one of my teammate's responses to a statement I made. "Jesus Christ, Suzanne! Why are you so damn hard on yourself?"

I was shocked into silence. Until that moment, I had no idea that I was hard on myself. It had never occurred to me that those around me would expect more or less of themselves than I did. It had never occurred to me that the thoughts in their heads about how they should have handed something in sooner, or done more analysis, or were having a bad hair day, might be any different than mine. This was my norm, and I just assumed it was everyone else's too, or at least everyone who might find themselves in an MBA program.

I can't say that I attacked the problem of being hard on myself at that very moment, but awareness is a powerful thing. It became something I examined as I moved forward in my life. I realized there was a voice in my head—and she wasn't very nice to me!

Since learning the principles of mindset, I have further become aware of and changed the language I use when speaking about myself, my accomplishments, and my "miss-takes." Generally, I am able to summon the inner self who speaks kindly and more appreciatively to me.

Sometimes, the twenty-eight-year-old "so darn hard" on herself Suzanne shows up. But she gets a lot less airtime in my head these days, and I work hard to counter-balance her by reframing what she has to say. If there is one thing I've learned in the process, it is that negative self-talk has never helped me to improve, to strive harder, or to succeed. Conversely, when I tell myself I've done a good job, done enough for the day, or that I should be proud of what I've achieved, it often encourages me to go the extra mile.

There are times I find myself at my desk, working toward finishing something but tempted to get up and get sidetracked. When I can muster the ability to tell myself how much I've gotten done, how close I am, and that I just have another twenty-to-thirty minutes until the project is complete, I can usually re-focus and get busy. Completing the project and thus creating the satisfaction that comes along with checking it off my to-do list.

Chastising myself has never had the same effect. I'm certain of that. The more positive my self-talk is, the more I stay focused on the projects that move my business forward faster. So positive self-talk and encouragement, here I come.

Do you ever think about how you talk to yourself? Do you use words and phrases you would never use on a friend, or someone else you love? This experience taught me that how I treat others starts with how I treat myself. I've seen that to be true in others as well.

There are people in my life who frequently talk about what those around them are doing wrong or find criticism in the smallest choices or elements of others' personalities. When I see this, what used to make me angry or caused me to look down upon them, now creates empathy. It gets me thinking that if they are so critical of others, what must that voice in their head be saying to them. It must be hard to live with.

As I sit here today writing, I can picture the face of the young man who startled me with his question. Twenty years later, I cannot remember his name. I wish we were connected so I could thank him for helping me open up a dialogue with myself. I think he'd find today that I am kinder both to myself and to those around me as a result.

32

THE BASEMENT

E arlier in this chapter, I wrote about positive emotions attracting and negative emotions repelling. Here's how this works in your business, and especially for your sales and marketing: positivity attracts.

When I'm working with clients, we look to understand what their ideal clients experience before working with them. Then we discuss what their clients will experience after working with them. The now is always worse, of course. That's why prospects will invest in the solution being offered. However, there are many ways to present people's challenges and the solutions.

Some marketers choose to use fear and negativity because it can work. Likely everyone reading this can remember, or has heard of, the famous "This is your brain, this is your brain on drugs" public service campaign from the late 1980s. (Aren't familiar? Do a search on YouTube as it's there.) This was a clear, negative campaign using fear to entice teenagers away from using cocaine. I learned on Mental-Floss.com that three years after the ad campaign began, The Partnership for a Drug-Free America announced a ten percent increase in the number of teenagers who believed even occasional use of cocaine was dangerous.

While this campaign worked, most individuals, consciously or not, like to be courted with positivity. We don't like it just because of the Law of Attraction; we like it because it's more pleasant. Consider the Farmers Insurance Group commercials that depict crazy things happening to homeowners. The events themselves are negative, but Farmers brings levity to home disasters, removing the negativity—at least in the commercials. Given that this ad campaign has continued for a number of years, I can only assume that it is doing very well for the Farmers. I know I always get a chuckle out of the campaign and appreciate its levity.

Knowing that positivity draws people in, and negativity repels them, I want to ooze positivity, light, and kindness. In doing so, I hope to attract others who ooze positivity, light, and kindness. Those are the people I want to be around. Of course, I am human, and therefore not always successful, but I work at it every day.

As a coach and consultant, it is easy to fall into the trap of putting down another coach or consultant's process. We may believe that we have the best process, or the only one that works. We may also be able to see with our trained eye exactly why another's program isn't working for some of their clients.

In light of what we know about positivity and negativity though, we should not speak ill of another's solution. Each of us comes to our own conclusion about what works for us, and, hopefully, we attract those who will also benefit from our process. Others will be served well by others and are not the right fit for us.

If you think about sales situations you've been in, you've likely experienced being drawn to positivity and repelled by negativity. A fairly recent experience rings true for me.

In late 2018, shortly after moving to Massachusetts, Kevin and I decided to partially finish our basement. We invited salesmen from two different companies to come to our home, discuss our desired plans, and provide a quote. Both companies did a great job of listening to what we wanted and reflecting it back to us. We had a nice rapport with both salesmen and their quotes were within five percent of each other. We ended up using the more expensive option. The decision to do so stemmed from one part of the experience.

The salesman for the more expensive company told us all about their solution: why it was fantastic, how it had a lifetime warrantee, why if our basement ever flooded, we would be okay. He focused on the positive attributes of the system, the installation process, the professional teams they used, and their excellent testimonials on every aspect of their solution.

The salesman for the less expensive company spent the bulk of his time with us telling us why the other company was bad. His attention was focused on the negatives of the other system, the poor service, and the laissez-faire attitude of the employees and contractors, and how his company had replaced finished basements from the other company due to dissatisfaction. While I enjoyed pleasantries with this salesman, when we got down to business, he really turned me off.

The best advice I can provide is to focus on the positivity of your own message. It is okay for your marketing message to communicate the frustrations potential clients are likely experiencing in "before working with you" language. However, be sure to follow these messages with how you solve those problems, not with how others don't.

The biggest impediment to sticking to a positive message rather than sharing why another's solution doesn't work is our own ego. We want to believe we are the best, the only, and that no one else can provide a solution as well as we can. In my experience, this is only the case when developing something completely revolutionary.

Most complex problems can be solved in several ways. Your solution, as great as it is, won't work for everyone. That fact is not about you. Don't let your ego tell you otherwise.

Instead, remove your ego from the equation and release the need to be right. You will be right for some, and you will not be right for others. This will often have to do with timing, and the mindset of the client. Don't worry. There are plenty of people out there you will be right for! There will also be plenty you will not be right for. It can be a bitter pill to swallow, but it is true. Release the ego part of your pursuit and know that those you serve will be served and that is what's most important.

33

INTERNALIZE THIS SECTION

M any parents speak about their children and say they learn more from their kids than they could ever teach them. That is because, to be a successful parent, we must keep learning. Our children develop. They have new and different needs, and present new and different challenges for us (*ahem*, sometimes daily!). Our businesses teach us too. They stretch us beyond our boundaries and force us to become the people who can take the next step. My business has done this for me. Likely yours has too for you.

I'm still learning about mindset and incorporating it more every day. Sometimes, I find myself needing to relearn, or at least be reminded, of what I already know. Always, I know that whatever is going on in my mindset is going to play out in my business and my life.

I do find, that the deeper my work on my mindset gets, the more I see its importance. Here are some things for you to consider based on what I shared in this chapter:

- What do you need to grow in yourself in order to grow in your business?

- Are there responsibilities, projects, or people you need to release in your business in order to grow?
- Are you aware of your conscious mindset?
- What do you need to do in order to counteract negative thoughts and feelings?
- What are the best activities for you to do to feel better on a regular basis?
- How would you describe your money mindset?
- How comfortable are you investing in yourself or your business?
- Do you have a gratitude practice? Do you connect it with achieving more?
- Do you struggle to forgive, or does it come easily to you? Would something positive come from forgiving someone in your life right now?
- Have you made mindset shifts related to your spouse, partner, or other long-term relationship? Are there some it would serve you to make?
- Has anyone ever said anything to you that changed the way you thought of your inner self?
- Would you speak to others the way your internal voice speaks to you?
- Do you currently have a positive approach to selling your services? Do you ever put others down or compare yourself in the sales process?

STRENGTH

34
———

STRENGTH

 It is worth remembering that the time of greatest gain in
terms of wisdom and inner strength is often that of
greatest difficulty.

— DALAI LAMA

I f you are a mother with her own business, we likely have a lot in
common. This is also true if you are not a mother but have a care-
giving and supportive role to anyone in your life. Sometimes our businesses must take a backseat to life. Just as people take leaves of
absence from their jobs, we at times need to be absent from our businesses. The difference is how we think others' feel about us taking the
time we need.

No one—who is sane—gives new mothers a difficult time for
taking time off after they give birth. Of course, businesses in the
United States provide less time off for new moms than almost
anywhere else in the civilized world, and short maternity leave has
become normalized here. Also normalized is the fact that sometimes

we need to take extended time away from work for other family issues: care-giving for a sick parent, personal illness, etc. Yet, somehow as entrepreneurs, we chide ourselves if we are not focused on building our businesses from day one until we decide to close or sell them.

Perhaps not everyone feels this way, but I certainly did when I needed to take a break. It has taken me a couple of years to feel that I don't need to explain my extended absence from my business. In truth, I still feel a bit like a failure because of it, but I'm committed to forgiving myself, someday.

It takes a lot of personal energy to run a business, and life events happen that take us away from be able to do so sometimes. What we learn as we grow is that creating systems in our business helps, as does bringing on support. But when we are on our own, if something tips the scales and we can't keep up, pausing is what usually happens. It's what happened to me.

35

OPPORTUNITY

In the fall of 2013, Kevin and I lived with our boys in suburban New Jersey. Kevin commuted daily to Manhattan where he worked in IT for a clothing retailer. He loved the work, but hated the commute, which took about an hour and a half each way *when* things went smoothly.

One night as we were getting ready for bed, he asked if I would ever consider moving to Vermont. He explained that a college friend had reached out that day about a job that was right up his alley.

"That's your dream job," I said, remembering back to an earlier conversation. When we were dating, Kevin told me of three New England companies he dreamed of working for because they would be solid jobs in idyllic locations.

I told him almost immediately that I would be open to moving to Vermont and that he should pursue the job. If the application process went anywhere, we would discuss a move more seriously. He applied, and soon we found ourselves making plans to move.

Both of us were extremely excited about the prospect of moving "out of the rat race." Manchester, Vermont is a lovely town, and the idea of raising our children there, skiing, hiking, and enjoying a slower pace of life, while having our money go further, enticed us. Kevin was excited about a thirty-minute commute.

36

CHOOSING TRANSITION

By early 2014, Kevin was working in Vermont while the boys and I wrapped up our lives in New Jersey. In addition to our move, both of us were going through work transitions. I realized that my virtual assistant business no longer served me in the way it once had and that it was time for me to step more fully into the business coaching I'd been yearning to do. I straddled the fence between the business that lit me up, and the one that paid the bills. All of our transitions were a bit scary, but we embraced them with excitement.

The move was more complicated than most. First, we moved into a rental house because we needed to sell the New Jersey property before purchasing a new home. Over the summer, we sold the New Jersey house, and bought and moved into our Vermont home.

We looked at our move to Vermont as permanent. We expected that our children would be raised there, at least throughout the thirteen years until they both graduated high school. As a result, we made our Manchester home our dream house. We updated the center hall colonial with new flooring, a classy powder room, and a kitchen to die for. We chose quality fixtures and cabinets, believing we would be there a good long time to enjoy them. Through my networking connections, I met a woman who was great with colors, and she ended up painting every single room in the house for us, including the window trim. She even painted an underwater mural for the boys' room.

We'd been in our newly renovated home about nine months when Kevin and I went to visit family for an engagement party in New Jersey. A few minutes into the car ride, Kevin broke some bad news to me. His friend, the one who had reached out to him about the job in Vermont, had been laid off that afternoon. Kevin had seen factions developing within the company resulting from new leadership. We both had a sense of dread, as we knew that Kevin's allegiances were on the wrong side of a growing tide. The news cast somewhat of a pall over our otherwise enjoyable visit to New Jersey.

A few weeks later, Kevin arrived home early from the office. Calmly, he told me his job had been eliminated. He had been invited to stay with the company, albeit at a lesser job and lower salary. His answer was required the next day. His boss knew quite well that he had just invited Kevin into the space between a rock and a hard place. There were no other jobs in the area that required his skills, or that would pay close to what he was making.

We reasoned that accepting the lesser position made sense. We hoped there would be a shift in the company that would allow us to stay. In our hearts, I believe we both knew this was the beginning of the end. Accepting the lesser job granted Kevin time and gave us a reasonable income while he looked for a new one.

At this stage, my coaching business was bubbling along. Some lovely opportunities for exposure had come my way, and new clients had followed. While my practice wasn't completely full, I felt pleased with the direction things were going in. I found that traveling outside of Vermont was key to me bringing in longer term, higher value clients, so I worked to do that whenever possible. I stopped taking new virtual assistant clients in an effort to keep my attention on my passion: coaching.

37

PANIC

I nterviews with a variety of companies followed Kevin's shift in job status. Unfortunately, so did insults from his boss, warnings from trusted colleagues, and a growing sense of dread. Ultimately, it took another nine months until I got a text from him indicating that day, a Thursday, would be his last day at the company.

"Bastards," was all I could think. The irony of living in a small town is that, when I received that text, I was sitting next to a woman whose husband's work cube was right next to Kevin's. One of her closest friends was the wife of the man who had just fired my husband.

Kevin is extremely good at what he does. He is conscientious, timely, thorough, and consistent. He is the well-oiled freight train that runs along-side my loop-de-loop rollercoaster. Sometimes being great at what you do doesn't matter. You can't fit a round peg into a square hole. No matter what Kevin did, he was not going to be the perfect right-hand guy to his boss.

In marketing and coaching, we talk about how, in some ways, there is no such thing as competition. People choose to work with those they connect with. That connection sometimes comes for very tangible, identifiable reasons. Other times, it was completely unexplainable.

There are coaches who have changed my life for the better. Yet, I have friends I deeply respect, who would say, "Yeah, I just could never really connect with her." These unexplainable connections or disconnections happen all the time. Kevin was not his Vermont boss's "guy" and never would be.

Being rejected can be a crushing experience, and more so when the rejection feels like a reflection on our ability to support our family or live out our dreams. We moved forward as a family and accepted that our time in Vermont would be short-lived, not a lifetime as we'd believed.

What you may not know about rural areas is that selling a home can take significantly longer than in more populated areas. Despite being recently overhauled at great expense, it took us almost a year to successfully sell our Vermont home.

During much of that year, we lived separately with Kevin, who had secured a new job, in New Jersey, and the boys and I in Vermont. Our goal was to allow the children to have consistency until we could purchase a new home where we wanted to settle. I maintained clients in my business but traveling to reach out to new ones didn't fit into the picture. Looking back, I know there is a lot more I could have done to bring clients in, but at the time, I just didn't have it in me emotionally.

The trials and tribulations—the energy of maintaining a long-distance relationship with my husband, the additional support my children needed, the maintenance required of a house on the market—all took their toll on me. And just the thought of moving, recreating personal and business networks, and settling our family in to a new home and school system felt overwhelming. Having already recently relocated, I knew exactly how much energy it would sap from me. This time, I wasn't nearly as excited about it.

After about a year of total chaos, two seemingly unrelated events rocked our world again. In the same week that we finally got an offer on our Vermont home, Toys "R" Us, where Kevin worked in New Jersey, announced that it would not be coming out of bankruptcy. Within forty-eight hours, we were released from the albatross of a home in a state where he couldn't find work and plunged once again into the shock of not knowing where we would move.

Have you ever had a panic attack? I'm not being figurative when I ask this. If you have, then you know how exceptionally scary they can be. I had experienced panic attacks before our move to Vermont, and wrongly believed I knew how to calm myself when one started.

It was March of 2018 when I learned I had no control over my panic attacks. Kevin continued working at Toys "R" Us a few weeks past their ill-fated announcement, leaving me in Vermont with the boys during the week. One Friday night, instead of expecting his arrival, I was running through my head what I needed to pack for a trip to New Jersey to celebrate my father-in-law's seventieth birthday.

Despite the many trips I'd taken alone with Stuart, Walter, and the dog, I felt anxiety rise in me as I considered organizing us and getting out the door the next morning. At bedtime, I snuggled with each of the boys, settled the house for the night, and retired to my room.

In the middle of the night, uncharacteristically, I awoke from a sound sleep. Getting up to go to the bathroom, I felt dizzy and short of breath. The logical side of my brain told me that I was having a panic attack and I needed to breathe calmly to let it pass. But this one felt different. I couldn't breathe my way through it. My chest felt tight.

I weighed the decision to call 911 or not. In my head, I debated whether I could actually be having a heart attack, or if I could confidently determine that the culprit was panic. I realized that if I was wrong, if there was something happening with my heart, my children could find me dead in my bed the next day. I dialed 911 and pushed the green button.

God bless the men from the ambulance who didn't make me feel crazy. God bless my friend Kim, who not only answered her phone at 3:30 a.m. but also came to my house within minutes, cared for my children, and picked me up from the hospital the next morning. God bless the numerous doctors I followed up with just to be certain there was nothing wrong with my heart, who also did not make me feel crazy.

Some friends asked me if I regretted calling 911, and when the bills rolled in, I had to consider whether I did. I don't. I'm glad I had the courage to put myself first in that moment and to be absolutely certain that my own silence or embarrassment wouldn't be my downfall.

There are women I've known who didn't take warning signs seriously and are no longer with us. Without question, there will be more. I'm here to tell you, that the bills and the embarrassment are well worth it. I'm pretty sure they are a lot easier to live through than an actual heart attack.

ACCEPTANCE

As I am recounting this, it is November of 2020. While I never would have thought I'd be thankful for the challenges Kevin and I faced as a result of our Vermont adventure, I can share without reservation that I am. Eight months into the coronavirus pandemic, I know that we, and our boys, are strong. We have gotten through some really sucky times.

Having each other, our health, and the love of friends and family we've pushed through many challenges. Every time there was an unlucky turn, luck and support followed. Knowing that past extraordinary challenges have turned out okay has helped me prop up my husband and my boys through this difficult time. Perhaps they would say the same of me.

Throughout the months, we've all taken turns at struggling with the strangeness. We will continue to do so. I do my best to stay focused on the good that will come from the struggle. My boys are learning what it means to live through adversity. They are finding ways to adjust to education that poses extra challenges. Their struggles today will make future expectations easier or at least will make them feel more achievable.

We've had our scares again through the pandemic about Kevin's job security. He is working for a retail company, and the pandemic was not a good time to be in retail. But in the scariest moments, the ones where I could see he was feeling the fear of letting us down, I have been able to confidently say, "We will be okay!" Each of our challenges has taught me this, the layered effect of them has helped me internalize it.

As a result of the adversity we've survived, I have much less fear around all that I want to accomplish. Now, I stretch myself in my business in ways I held back on for years. I have accepted my fear for what it is: a set of thoughts in my head about what could happen. I've used my experience as a counterbalance to show myself that when bad things happen, good things come from them. And ultimately, those horrible events don't seem so bad.

During all the chaos we lived through as a family, nothing ever got as bad as the feared outcome in my imagination. The saying, "That which does not kill us makes us stronger" is a cliché, and yet so very true.

So, the next time you are faced with something that seems like the worst thing that could happen, remember, it likely won't get as bad as you are imagining. If it does, you will come out of it stronger than you ever dreamed possible. Accept the situation as life, in this moment. The next moment will be different, probably better.

Having said this, know that you should and will mourn your losses. I believe one of the reasons I have my current perspective is that I took time to mourn all of our losses. They were plentiful.

Before Kevin lost his Vermont job, when I saw the impending doom, I allowed myself to feel the sadness of leaving the home we had so beautifully redone. There were times when he was off at work and the boys were off at school that I would walk through the house, my attention focused on the details we'd painstakingly decided upon, memorizing them. I wanted to be able to look back on the beauty we had created and enjoy it for the experience.

Even as I continued to connect with new people and make new friends in our small Vermont town, I accepted that the closeness I felt to them would be emotional, but soon my proximity to them would change.

I remember moments where the resistance and fear began to rise in my body, where I would feel the panic building. One day at my kitchen table with my back to the window overlooking beautiful rolling green mountains, I closed my eyes and started to repeat over and over again to myself, "In this moment, all is well. In this moment, all is well."

I'm sure my meditation lasted only a couple of minutes, but it felt like forever before my body started to accept my words, for my heart rate to slow, and my breath to ease. I thought about the table I held onto, the room I was in, the air I could breathe. The fact that my children were safely at school learning, knowing they were coming home to a loving environment. Then I moved on with my day.

When Kevin's job ended and we listed our home for sale, I mourned the loss of the money we had invested. I mourned that we would not recoup our investment, a step crucial for moving beyond it. We often associate mourning with death, but sometimes we need the chance to mourn life experiences that will never come to fruition. Some might say that mourning the loss of money is materialistic, but we attach meaning to it and sometimes our worth. I believe if we could all allow ourselves to mourn a bit more freely, rather than judging ourselves for it, we'd be a healthier society.

Loss of any kind creates an impact on one's life, and we need to take the time to integrate that into our expectations and perspective. Otherwise, we continue to carry the feelings of loss through everything else we do. When we can't leave those feelings behind, they weigh us down making everything seem more difficult. Feel your feelings. Accept yourself for having them. Only then will you be able to decide if you want to keep having them, or if you want to feel a different feeling.

Each time our family experienced a shift or change to our plans, I felt as though the rug had been pulled out from under me. But I learned acceptance was the only way through. Resistance would only make the situation more difficult.

39

GRACE

We moved into our new home in Massachusetts at the end of August 2018. We had less than two weeks to get ourselves reasonably settled and prepare the boys for starting at their new schools.

After a couple of years of chaos, my unwavering focus was to feel settled. I got everything possible done for the boys before school started and then worked hard to create the systems I needed in the house. Our new home was newly constructed, which was a new experience for me. So little things, like an extra shelf in the laundry area or hooks on the backs of doors, were needed.

I quickly familiarized myself with all the organization products available at Target, Walmart, Loews, and Home Depot. I hung artwork and focused on unpacking boxes. For about six weeks, I was relentless.

By early October, the house started to feel like home, and we were adjusting to life in our new spot. I finally took a breath and considered the future.

I walked around my family room, looking out the windows at the houses of my new neighbors. I peered at the sky, and I asked myself, "Okay, now what do you want?" To my dismay, I had no idea. We had been through such a long slog, and my wants had felt irrelevant throughout the process. I couldn't seem to identify my own desires.

All I could identify in that moment was how very alone and exhausted I felt. I knew more than anything that I needed women friends around me. I missed the simplicity of dropping my boys off at their Vermont school, running into some moms, and joining them at the local coffee spot adjoining the bookstore.

I grieved for the ease of those times and for the losses that come along with the excitement of something new. I reminded myself that my new neighbors were incredible, and friendly, and that we'd already begun socializing with many of them. We also had a set of dear friends in our new town that I'd known for years.

I realized that my overall feeling was one of complete burnout. The left side of my brain told me, "It's time to get back to working on your business, Suzanne." I'd handled the move. I was free from the five-days-a-week single motherhood role. We were a family again. The right side of my brain hung up its "gone fishing" sign, not an ounce of creativity remained.

During the weeks that followed, I did what was necessary for my family, and not much else. I napped when I felt tired. Walked with my dog while listening to audio books and spent a lot of hours curled up on my couch playing stupid games on my phone.

As the weather cooled down, I pulled out my knitting and decided on a number of projects to make as Christmas gifts. After Thanksgiving, I baked Christmas cookies, delivering some to our neighbors and mailing boxes to friends and family.

These activities soothed my soul and helped me begin to get my creative juices flowing again. During Christmas week, I felt a glimmer of joy about my business again. I dreamed of creating an entrepreneurial network in my new area.

Through my creativity, I released the baggage I'd carried, and my energy began to emerge again. After New Year's Day, when my boys returned to school and my husband went to work, I felt like myself again. Actually, I felt even better. For the first time in a long time, I was excited about the future. Every part of my body was filled with anticipation.

This was the beginning of a new phase for me. It came as a direct result of the kindness and compassion I'd shown myself throughout the fall and holiday season. I allowed myself to feel what I needed to, and to nurse my emotional creativity back to health.

Since then, there have been times I've begun to feel a little bit of burnout. This was especially true at the beginning of the COVID shutdown when the world felt entirely topsy-turvy. Now I know to invoke the lessons I've learned: to slow down, to allow myself extra time and space, to do what makes me feel creative. Doing so helps me to find my energy again and to keep it positive.

40

LEARNING

Each phase of our multi-state moves, and jobless experiences taught me about myself: my capabilities and limitations. Of course, the limitations were the part I liked learning about the least! While you will never have the same set of experiences as I did, you are living a life and building a business simultaneously. Both will throw you curveballs. There will be many times that life and business will pull you in opposite directions and you'll feel that one is holding you back from the other. Usually, you'll feel that life is holding you back from success in your business.

If I'd been able to see all this for myself sooner, I think I would have saved myself a lot of heartache. I spent years feeling wretched about myself because I didn't have the emotional energy to be the business-woman I wanted to be and knew I could be. My perception was that I was a failure because I could tell other people to market consistently but couldn't—for a time—do it myself.

One of the most important things I've learned is to accept where I am and start again as soon as I can. Too often, I've found myself fretting about what I didn't get done because of the needs of my family. The needs of my family were important, even if they were as simple as lunch being delivered to school, or an extra trip to the grocery store for cupcake ingredients. The fretting was what I could have done without.

Sitting around thinking about the work you didn't get done is of no value. Calling a friend to vent is fine. Calling five is a distraction. Understanding yourself well enough to know what you really need to get back on track is an imperative part of building a successful business. It comes with trial and error. Sometimes it comes from a kick in the pants from a coach or a friend who knows you close to as well as you know yourself.

I've learned that if my family is in chaos, it will affect my work. I will be the one to cancel appointments, have plans blow up in my face, and to feel crunched at the end of the day in order to deliver on promises. This outcome is the result of my role in our family, a role I've chosen and to which I am deeply committed. For my business, this means I cannot ever intentionally pack my schedule. I must leave space for the little daily requirements that crop up: the cupcakes, the rides to play dates, the additional trip to school to deliver a forgotten homework assignment.

There was a time that I wouldn't have created this space for myself. I allowed others' needs to dictate my schedule. Now, I regularly block a day on my calendar if I feel it is beginning to get too full of appointments, knowing that I can always fill the time with work or a personal commitment. Doing so allows me the balance I need to manage my family without putting myself into a tailspin.

Occasionally, I slip back into the space of not leaving myself enough time. I accept one too many appointments or commit myself to one too many deliverables. Every single time, I pay for it. Most often, over commitment crushes my confidence because I know I have no one else to blame.

There are also times when the little family challenges become bigger, and I accept that my family's requirements may go beyond the space I have left myself. It took me a very long time to be okay with this. As the Borg from Star Trek once said, "Resistance is futile." The longer I resist and push to maintain "business as usual," the more it will become derailed. Either the pressure will get to me and will negatively impact how I handle the family situation, or I will go down the mental rabbit hole of feeling like a failure because I can't keep everything together at the same time. Both paths lead to the same outcome: it takes me longer to get back to business with the positive energy I need for it. Instead, in a state of acceptance, I can handle what's required of me as a mother and wife, allowing myself to return to my role as a business owner more quickly.

If you take one piece of advice from this book, take this: putting yourself down in any way will never help you build a business. It is okay to take a break, to make mistakes, and to change course. It is okay to let the needs of your family or someone else you love become more important than your business to you for a time. Forgive yourself for your choices and pick up where you left off. Judgment is a waste of time and energy.

The break from my business has officially been over for a couple of years. I finally feel that I'm moving forward, not making up lost ground. I still find myself wishing that I'd done more to build it during these times of transition, but just as I accepted the life challenges then, I accept where my business is now. In this moment, all is well.

41

INTERNALIZE THIS SECTION

Whether your experience is as complicated as moving twice in a few years to support your spouse's career, or as simple as running to the grocery store for cupcake mix, life will create challenges for your business. As with so many things, preparation, organization, and structure are what will enable you to continue to grow or hold you back.

One of the biggest lessons from my experiences is that having support in my business for actions that don't need to be done by me eases the burden and enables me to keep going more consistently. Another is accepting each situation for what it is and forgiving myself when something negative is self-created.

Here are some things you may want to consider:

- Have you ever taken an extended break from working your business? How do you feel about it now? Is it a source of frustration or forgiveness for you?
- What opportunity have you taken that didn't work out the way you though it would? What are your feelings around that experience?
- Have panic, anxiety or depression impacted you and as a

result your business? Do you have the support you need around them if they resurface?

- Are there life experiences you have trouble accepting? Is it possible you haven't allowed yourself to mourn them?
- Have you ever found yourself unable to tap into your own desires? What is the worst burnout you've ever felt and how did you overcome it?
- Do you know what you need to do to recover from burnout and to get your creative juices flowing again?
- When life gets in the way of business how do you handle it? Do you have a plan in place that enables you to recover both in terms of your schedule and your emotional needs?

COMMUNITY

COMMUNITY

 Surround yourself with only people who are going to lift
you higher.

— OPRAH WINFREY

We are all members of communities. We live in them, grow up in them, shift in and out of them as necessary. We worship in them, shop in them, and play music in them. With the advent of the Internet, we can find a community for just about any aspect of our lives we wish. A community can help us blossom into the best person we can be, or it can be what stunts our growth and keeps us from personal development.

From the time we are very small children, we learn to navigate them, identify those we like and don't like. We make choices around them.

Communities have helped me to create my life and business as they are today. They have taught me who I want to be and influenced my values. Sometimes they have even saved me from failure.

43

GOLDEN RULE OR GOLDEN RETRIEVER?

Maya Angelou said, "People will forget what you did, but people will never forget how you made them feel." I can pretty much guarantee that my father had no idea who Maya Angelou was, but he was an expert at making people feel special. His genuine interest in people shined through in everything he did. He wanted to know those around him and was curious about their lives, their interests, and their families.

In fact, it was extremely rare that I heard him say anything negative about anyone he really knew. He looked for the good. I often joke that I get my Golden Retriever qualities from my dad: if people are nice to me, I like them. It doesn't occur to me not to.

In my twenties, I recall dating a young man who said something about making sure my dad liked him. I laughed and told him that he didn't have anything to worry about with my dad. Mom would be the one to really give him the once over. Not that she is horribly discerning, either.

Later, when I was dating my husband, I told him what my father's best friend thought of him was far more important than my dad's direct impression. Dad would like him, but if Uncle Rich had reservations, then he was in trouble.

My dad's interest in people sometimes embarrassed my mother. He would talk to waitresses and ask them all about their lives, background, and families. My mother would sit next to him, rolling her eyes, impatiently watching the diners at other tables trying to get our waitresses' attention quietly telling my father not to "grill" her.

Almost always, the waitresses were pleasant and warm, knowing that this was the guy who would pay the bill and decide upon their tip. Dad wasn't creepy in his questions, just thorough. He carried a pocket calendar with him, the same style year after year, that he took notes on. Often, he'd write little notes down about the waitresses so that when he returned to the restaurant he could check in about their earlier topics of conversation.

Dad's skill at making people feel good extended beyond those in front of him; he was excellent at keeping in touch. Family friends tell me that they could always count on his birthday phone call to check in and see how they were doing. He spent hours every day in the tufted chair in his office reaching out to people just to connect and to catch up.

One of Dad's favorite things to do was to have friends visit us in New Hampshire at the lake. The first summer we owned the house, he booked the guest room as though we owned a bed and breakfast. Friends left in the morning and new ones arrived that evening. This only happened one summer before my mother put her foot down about it.

Dad loved to share all he had with people, whether it was wine, the offer of a boat ride, an introduction, or time for a visit, he gave freely. Mom supported all of his inclinations, happily hosting dinner parties, overnight guests, and other gatherings.

Throughout my childhood, I'd find myself sitting at the top of our stairs after bedtime listening to my parents and their friends. Chatter, laughter, and the clinking of crystal glasses would carry throughout the house emanating from the adult-only dinner party in the dining room. My father's bellowing laughter often followed friends' storytelling and the giggling of my mother and the other women.

Years later, one evening in Vermont, my house was swarming with people. Five or six couples and all of their children had joined us for a last-minute potluck dinner gathering. A friend stopped me in my kitchen as the dog ran by following one of the low-to-the-ground children with a plate full of chips.

"How do you do this?" She asked. "I would be a nervous wreck if this was happening in my house right now! Aren't you worried they are going to tear the place apart?"

"Oh no," I responded. "This is how I grew up. My parents entertained all the time. Besides, all of our furniture already needs recovering, and the worst they can do is spill juice. I have a couple glasses of wine and choose not to worry about it!"

My parents' genuine appreciation for socializing and developing relationships taught me a lot about how to build a wonderful community of people around me. When I was younger, I took this effortless learning for granted. The more life experience I have, the more I value it. I realize I am exceptionally lucky for the way I grew up and the parents I have.

44

OH, SNAP!

As a wife and mother, I needed other women who knew what it was like to step through the phases of motherhood. I can't imagine surviving without this camaraderie.

When Stuart was a baby, I struggled to understand his schedule. A friend told me to write down his feedings. That simple suggestion—from an experienced mom to a new one—helped me to understand his needs and what to expect from him. At the time, my sleep deprived brain needed the support of that list more than I realized, and I likely wouldn't have come to that idea on my own.

After we moved to Vermont, I remember the first play date my boys had. The other mom and I discovered quickly after meeting that we each had first grade and pre-K boys. She invited us over, soon becoming one of my closest local friends.

As my children grew, my "mom communities" have supported me in so many ways. Friends have watched my boys while I've run to the store. They've taken them for an afternoon when I needed a break or driven them to a sports practice or birthday party when I couldn't clone myself. Most importantly, they've listened while I cried about an issue we just couldn't seem to get beyond.

These seemingly small moments add up and make that difference of feeling supported throughout our journeys. Of course, there are big moments that crop up, too.

When my boys were two and four years old, we were visiting my parents for Christmas week and decided to take the kids ice-skating. Upon arrival at a resort which offered all kinds of outdoor winter activities, we learned that the ice-skating rink wasn't quite frozen enough due to recent warmer than usual weather. To make the best of the situation, we elected instead to take them snow tubing.

Our younger son, Walter, was a bit of a daredevil at the time, and Stuart, our older son, was much more cautious. This dynamic created a challenge as we prepared to head up the hill for the first time. Stuart wanted no part of snow tubing. Walter was eager to get moving. Like many parents would have, we elected to split up. I headed up the lift with Walter and Kevin stayed behind with Stuart, attempting to coax him into trying it, "just this once."

Having waited in line at the bottom of the hill, and then again at the top for our turn, Walter and I finally got our first chance to slide down the hill in our tubes. What happened immediately following that changed the next few months for our family.

As I stepped out of my tube to help Walter out of his, my foot slipped on the icy surface of the crushed and smoothed out snow. I heard a snap, felt a horrible pain in my ankle and landed on the ice. I looked around for someone to help me, made eye contact with a man sitting nearby in a chair, and then with Walter. Then I put my head down on the tube and passed out.

As I became cognizant of people around me, and the fact that I had fainted, I told the gathering crowd that my husband was at the bottom of the lift line with our other son. Of course, by then Kevin had succeeded in getting Stuart to give snow tubing a try, and we waited for them to slide down the side of the mountain.

I broke my ankle that morning. While this injury would be a hassle for anyone, it was a disaster for the mother of two small children. Worse still, it was my right ankle, making driving impossible at a time when my children's day-care was twenty-five miles from our house, and Kevin's commute was ninety minutes away in the opposite direction.

We spent a lot of money on babysitters in the coming months. Friends and family swooped in to help take me to doctor appointments and to make meals for us. I will be forever grateful to each of them. But of that time, the strongest memory I have is of the day my neighbor Alicia took both my boys to her house for hours to play with her son. It was the first time that anyone who wasn't family, watched my children without being paid to do so. I remember them leaving the house together and me sobbing at the sense of relief I had and the gratitude for the kindness she showed me.

Without the other moms in my life, I can't imagine where I would be. The support and love my friends have shown me have carried me through so many challenges. They've made a difference to my life, my business, and my state of mind. I'm grateful to every single one of them.

45

A TRIBE OF ROLLER COASTER RIDERS

There is another community I needed too: my entrepreneurial one. Growing a business is a lot like growing a child. There are moments where things come so naturally you don't have to think about them. There are others when it feels like no matter what you do nothing works and you feel like you'll never find the right answer.

As the owner of a micro-business, I spend a great deal of time completely alone thinking about my business and working on developing it. In that vacuum, I can convince myself of anything because there is no one there to check me. I can work myself into a pretzel over-complicating an idea that will never work. I can also convince myself that there is something wrong with an elegant solution to a problem. Having friends and colleagues who understand this dilemma and all its inherent challenges is game changing.

There is not a chance as an entrepreneur that you will feel confident all the time. There is not a chance that you won't sometimes feel like you've chosen to live on a roller coaster instead of a steady-moving reliable train. Having one's own business is a daily challenge and creates the need for constant personal and professional growth.

In my experience, there is a lot of insecurity along the way. The fear of taking a step in any direction can be paralyzing. In the early years of entrepreneurship, my response to this was to want to talk issues or ideas out with someone. My challenge was being surrounded by train riders.

Train riders live in a totally different way. They don't understand our need for the highs or the sweeping turns. They don't understand that the lows make the highs even better. They definitely don't understand that when we roller coaster riders step off at the end of each ride, all we can think is, "I want to go again!"

My train riding friends and family don't understand why I would want to work so hard when I could just go get a job making good money. If I had a dollar for every time my mother has said, "I just hate to see you so stressed all the time," I'd be a wealthy woman. It wasn't that my train riding community doesn't want me to succeed at my dreams; they simply couldn't understand my dreams.

Entrepreneurs need people around them who see their dreams and say, "Awesome! Let's talk about how you can make that happen!" We need to be surrounded by those who see that we are right on the precipice of huge expansion and all we need is a little nudge. "You've got this." "You can totally do this, Suzanne." "That other person who's done this…she doesn't know more than you, she just did it first and has shown you it can be done." The ones who say this stuff, they are your tribe. As you find them along your journey, it is critically important for you to build relationships with them.

Ten years into entrepreneurship, I feel extremely lucky to have developed many supportive tribes. They all help love me into better versions of myself.

Some came into my life before I knew I would take the entrepreneurial path. Others came along because of it. My friend Anne and I met in college when we pledged the same sorority. With the exception of the fact that we both have our own businesses, she and I live opposite lives. She is unmarried, has no kids, and lives in a major urban center. She's a top real-estate agent with a committed business partner. We've been building our friendship for almost thirty years and usually speak every week, sometimes more than once. Anne always knows what I need to hear, good, bad, or ugly. She listens intently. She calls me on my bullshit. She loves me unconditionally.

This was not always the case. When we first met in college, I had no idea that she couldn't stand me. I have always been extremely outgoing and an open book. There's almost nothing you could ask me that I wouldn't tell you the honest answer to. I was loud, and very comfortable being the center of attention.

Anne is guarded. She is warm and friendly, and extremely socially adept, but she doesn't let just anyone into her inner circle. Years after we became friends, she told me that she avoided walking through my dorm often electing to walk outside in sub-zero temperatures just to avoid me. Now, we laugh about it all the time.

One time, walking across campus with a group of sorority sisters, Anne said to me, "Well, we aren't really friends." I thought this was a bit odd, as I felt we were becoming friends if we weren't already but didn't let it bother me. I had no idea that she only put up with me because of some mutual friends.

Apparently, I wore her down over time. She found that, in going a bit deeper with me, there was something more than the brash party girl she initially saw. Thank goodness she took a second look. She has given me some of the sagest advice in my lifetime. I can't imagine how different my life would look if she wasn't in it.

While I began collecting some special friends and tribe mates before, I really learned about creating a tribe when I went to my first entrepreneurial conference in April 2011. I had been struggling for six months to figure out business on my own when a friend posted on her Facebook profile an offer from her business coach.

The offer was free, and I snapped it up. Welcome to the funnel, Suzanne! I moved swiftly through it and ended up at the *Get More Clients* event in Stamford, Connecticut, spending three days with Fabienne Fredrickson, a room full of other entrepreneurial women, and a few great men, who had also made their way through Fabienne's funnel.

One of the messages conveyed at the event was the importance of having a tribe that understands you. Fabienne highlighted exactly how difficult it is to go it alone in entrepreneurship and her words were absolute truth for me.

From that event, I created my first entrepreneurial tribe. There were women with whom I genuinely connected in Stamford, and we followed up with each other afterward. Like Laura Clark, who teaches women to tap into their hearts and understand what their soul is telling them. Laura inspired me many times to think, "What would Laura do?" I realized that she would tell me to ask myself what my own next, right step is. Or like Jeannie Spiro, whose years of study and hard work have shown me what is possible for a New England mom who wants to crush a business without having it crush her life. Or like Morna Golletz, who connected with me over our mutual love for quilting before she became the client who put my virtual assistant business on the map. These women and I supported each other and grew our businesses alongside each other. They were among the first to tell me what they saw in me, how capable they thought I was. They encouraged me to grab whichever brass ring I told them I was considering and gave me great advice along the way about how to do it.

I followed Fabienne and learned from her on different levels for years. Many people I met through her community are still my tribe today. They root for me, and I root for them, even when we do similar work and might be considered competitors. When I think of Fabienne and her work, I am deeply grateful for everything I have learned from her. The impact of her teaching goes well beyond my business. She has changed my life for the better.

46

IT'S IN THE DNA

W hen I learned I was moving to a Boston suburb, one of my prevailing thoughts was that if I didn't find the right women's networking group there, I would start one. When I mentioned this to friends, they would ask, "How will you know it's right?"

My answer was always the same, "When I attend a meeting, it will not just help me create a network, it will feed my soul."

A few months after our move, a friend suggested, more than once, that I check out a women's group called Polka Dot Powerhouse. My first response was, "Polka Dot what? What the hell kind of a name is that?" In January 2018, after much prodding I attended a meeting, and immediately realized my friend was right. I walked in, and women practically ran to me to make me feel welcome. Then I discovered a gal I'd known for several years, with whom I'd loosely kept in touch with via Facebook, was the meeting's speaker. Within minutes, I knew I'd found the right group. These were my people.

At first, I didn't understand why I felt so at home among my new "Dot Sisters," but as I learned more about the organization, it became clear to me. I received a membership welcome packet, which included a bookmark that said:

"It doesn't make a difference what your history is, the kind of purse you carry, or how much money you have.

"It doesn't matter to us the kind of car you drive or your religious or political views.

"Just know that as long as you come in an authentic, positive, no-drama, action-forward way, and are willing to both give and receive, you will be accepted and appreciated here.

"That's the world I want to live in and that is the type of sisterhood I belong to."

The bookmark includes a picture of the Polka Dot Powerhouse founder, Shannon Crotty. Shannon created a very clear vision of the organization she wanted to create. In doing so, she attracted women of strong character who supported this vision by actively participating in it. The overall result was women who listen, who choose to truly connect with one another, and who have kind words for each other. It is in the DNA of the group.

Fabienne's community evolved from her vision too. I didn't know when I entered her vortex that I was stepping into a group of kindred spirits. It wasn't evident to me back in 2011 that the business direction I sought came with a side of learning to take personal responsibility and opening to enlightenment, but it did.

As you find your own tribes, look to their leaders. They will tell you everything you need to know about whether their community is a fit for you. The answer is not simply about what they teach, or demographics of the group. It is far more likely to be in the unseen characteristics of its make-up.

The tribes I've found are not simply great at providing me with an 'atta girl' when I need one. They are willing to go a step further and show me their expectations of me. They encourage me while also helping me to stretch myself. Because of them, I try new things I'd previously just thought about. When I fail, which goes right along with living on the roller coaster, they give me a safe place to land. Then, they lift me up and encourage me to ride again.

There is no way my business would be where it is today, or that I would be writing this book without the love, support, and belief in me my tribe emanates. And when I fearfully put the book out into the world, I know they will be among the first to say well done. This is what having a tribe means. It is a necessity for everyone, but especially for those of us who choose the rollercoaster.

47

MIND THE GAPS

The MBA program I graduated from is specifically known for its focus on entrepreneurship. On the first day of the program, we were taught two tenets of entrepreneurship: ambiguity is your friend, and you are only as good as your team. The first-year curriculum was the same for every student and focused on providing a basic understanding of all a business owner might encounter. We studied everything from creatively working in teams to basic statistics. Grades, instead of being doled out in the traditional A-B-C format, were delivered based on an understanding of professional standards. When we received a "Meets Professional Standards" or "MPS," we let out a sigh of relief and moved on to our next project or course. Our saying was, "No stress...MPS."

The second-year curriculum allowed for us to specialize in our own areas of interest. Usually, students chose areas of strength as their focus area. Most students elected to lean into what they are good at. I decided to challenge myself.

It did not go well.

Most of my courses were in marketing, my strength and interest. However, I was under the mistaken impression that I needed to learn more about accounting in order to be successful. I've always been interested in finance and somehow made the decision that getting into the weeds of accounting might help me flourish in this area.

Second year accounting was a class I never should have taken. I struggled the entire time despite considerable effort. My saving grace was the team-based project that made up a large portion of our grade. Two of my friends were in the class and naturally we joined together to form a team.

As the semester drew to a close, the professor asked me to meet her in her office. "Suzanne," she said, "I know you have been really trying hard in this class."

I confirmed what she already knew and assured her that I was digging deep trying to understand the material. At this point, she handed me back my latest test with the abysmal grade on the front of it. It was not the first.

"It's very good that you selected Cindy and Jim to be your team members on the project," she continued.

"I know!" I exclaimed. "They really seem to know what they are doing. They are trying to help me along, but I'm afraid I'm not bringing a lot to the team."

"You're not planning to take the next-level accounting class, are you?" she asked.

"I considered it but decided it probably wasn't a good idea," I answered.

"It isn't. Suzanne," she replied, "if you were not on the team with Jim and Cindy, you would be failing this class. I strongly recommend to you that you focus on other areas." The pity in her eyes now had an element of pleading as well. I promised her not to continue my accounting career and thanked her for being so kind before I left her office.

Six months later at our graduation ceremony, Jim received the accounting award. Both he and Cindy have gone on to twenty-plus year careers where deep knowledge of accounting principles plays a key role. I stick to business strategy and marketing. This is the place I belong. It's where my strengths lie.

While I did not master accounting principles my second year of business school, I did learn a lesson that has stuck with me and became far more important in my career and personal development. There will always be things you are not great at. When you identify them, you have two choices: the first is to torture yourself into trying to get better, and the second is to fill the gap by finding someone to help. The most important thing is to find people you can trust to support you and your business in these areas; preferably people who are really good at them. That lesson has been a lifesaver to me, and critical to the development of my business. Apparently that lesson about building the right team on day one of B-school was an important one—and what a gift it turned out to be.

Minding the gaps has shown up in other ways, too. One of the things I'm not very good at is being consistent. It is a muscle I continue to work on building in my personal life, and in my professional life. It's also ironic because I so often talk about the importance of consistency in our marketing. Perhaps I know of its importance because of how much I've struggled with it myself.

For a long time, I didn't know how much of a weakness this was for me. I figured it out when, for the third year in a row, I claimed it as the number one most important thing I needed to do in the coming year, right around January first. When you get to year three claiming the same goal as your New Year's Resolution, it's difficult not to recognize it as an area you need to take a deeper look at.

As I experienced in my accounting class, believing that I can push myself to improve at an area of weakness hasn't worked out so well for me. However, I've discovered that with perseverance we can find ways to overcome weaknesses with external motivations. By expanding the community of women working in my business, I've created systems that keep me organized, and provide hard deadlines, thus improving my otherwise horrible consistency.

For example, if I want my newsletter to go out weekly, I've got to get the proper materials to my assistant by our mutually arranged deadline. Deadlines help me a lot, as does having someone expecting stuff from me. When I am working alone and have no community around me, it is extremely easy to let myself down by not sticking to a deadline. But a shift happens when I know I would be letting someone else down. I have great team members, and I don't want them to get frustrated by a leader who doesn't stick to the plan. I ask them to make commitments to me, so I need to keep my commitments to them.

Of course, I learned this lesson of external motivation the hard way. For a number of years, I had someone helping me to get a newsletter out every week like clockwork. At a certain point, she decided to take a full-time job and stopped working for me. Can you guess what happened?

I didn't jump right in to find someone else to help me with the work. I decided I could do it myself. Quickly my very consistent newsletter went haywire. It wasn't until I found someone else to come in and support me again that I began sending it with any regularity.

As a result, I lost people from my list. I lost their engagement, ended up in their SPAM filter, and likely became someone they didn't remember. When I finally engaged someone new to help, I had a lot of ground to make up.

Social media was a second area that I've found having support was key. Before I hired a team member for this, I posted, but not regularly, and not with a plan in place around what I was sharing. Bringing someone on to help me made me think ahead and provide direction. In addition to creating consistency, getting support made me more thoughtful and more strategic. It also increased my exposure and helped me get more clients.

One of the most critical gaps I've filled was with bookkeeping. I've been through a series of bookkeepers in my ten plus years in business. The best are those who take the time to think about my business and push me to take the next growth step. There have been times when I wanted someone to "just do the numbers" so that I could submit my tax return on time. And I have to admit that's what I thought I was looking for when I hired my current bookkeeper.

In truth, having Connie Jo Miller of Enigma Bookkeeping Solutions on board in my business gives me needed accountability—for the numbers I am achieving, or not. At the end of each month, I think about the fact that someone else's eyes are on that part of my business. There is someone there to say, "You struggled this month, huh?" or "Wow, you had a great month!"

Knowing that she is an active participant in my business means a lot to me. I am a people person, a relationship person. I'm also a Leo and we like recognition and attention. My regular conversations with Connie Jo about my books are a driver for me to focus that much more on consistency and on financial success.

These are just three ways I've expanded the community within my business. Filling these gaps helps me overcome my own weaknesses and allows me to focus on the stuff I'm good at instead of chastising myself for struggling. While investing in support can be a big, scary step, it can also be what lights a fire and helps you move beyond your struggle areas.

48

WHAT JFK SAID

L ike any other relationships, those with members of your tribe require building, nurturing, love, and attention. They cannot be taken for granted.

We have all experienced the fun and ease of developing a new relationship. A visit over coffee, in person or via Zoom, can lead to a lively discussion of common interests, concerns, frustrations, and life experiences. These conversations are only the start though. They are the equivalent of first dates—wonderful and exciting, but a blink when compared with what goes into building a fifty-year marriage.

Creating relationships that truly support you takes time. It requires regular interaction and an emotional connection. None of which comes without effort.

My parents understood the nurturing of friendships near and far. Dad was especially adept at it, and sometimes enlisted Mom as his social secretary. A common December refrain in our household was, "Hey Alyce, how are the Christmas cards coming along?" Followed by my mother's reply, from our kitchen table strewn with boxes of cards, "I'm on the Ms!" She hand-wrote notes on every single one of them.

To stay connected and keep relationships going, I carve out time in my schedule. I write notes, paper and electronic. I send cards and letters. I make phone calls. I take an extra moment to make a meaningful comment on a social media post, rather than just clicking a heart or a like. Every day, I wish I could do more of each. Most days, I do little or none. But every morning it is in my heart to reach out to someone I care about, someone whose relationship with me is meaningful. When I put my head on my pillow at night and I have, I end the day a little bit happier for the connection and satisfied with the fact that I know I'm doing my best.

Creating a tribe of supporters means being a supporter yourself. Sharing what others are doing and loving them up for doing it can be so easy and take very little time. Yet, it means so much. Simple acts like commenting on the social media posts of other business owners you know or sharing them if they could benefit your community go a long way toward building relationships. If you want to build a valuable tribe, keep in mind as you go through your day, how you can provide value to them.

John F. Kennedy said, "Ask not what your country can do for you —ask what you can do for your country." Consider your tribe in the same manner. Above all, keep top of mind what you can do for others, rather than what they can do for you. If you do this, you will likely have a stream of goodwill coming your way, just when you need it most.

49

SURVIVOR

I met my husband on Match.com. I like to joke that you can find anything you want on the Internet. He was not my first Match.com date, a number of others preceded him. Some I liked, but they weren't interested. Others, I chose not to pursue. One stands out in my memory as the worst date of my life.

We'd arranged our meeting over email and agreed to meet at a Macaroni Grill between our homes. I'd always thought first dates were fun and easy, believing that I could talk to just about anyone for a couple of hours. This guy made me think watching paint dry would be more interesting.

We couldn't find anything in common to talk about. Only about thirty minutes into our date, we talked about television shows, and we didn't even like any of the same ones. I particularly remember this because his favorite was *Survivor*. He droned on and on about it. I had zero interest and found his episode recounting tedious.

One of my rules for first dates was not to go to the movies. I knew I wouldn't get to know someone sitting next to him in a theater. This date was so bad that when he suggested a movie after dinner, I said yes—anything so that I didn't have to listen to him babble on anymore!

Despite feeling I can speak with, and connect to, just about anyone,

I've had similar business networking experiences. I've entered a networking meeting and known almost immediately it wasn't the crowd for me. I've found myself in one-on-one meetings wondering, "What the heck am I doing talking to this person?" It is rare, but it happens to all of us.

I've had many women tell me that they can't stand the structure of certain networking organizations while others tell me that joining the same one was the best thing that ever happened for their business. No community is right for everyone, and no one person is going to make a genuine connection with everyone she meets. That's okay!

Remember, just as you shouldn't keep dating someone you don't like, you shouldn't keep networking with people when there is no spark. Accepting the spark doesn't exist doesn't make either party bad it simply means there is a bad match.

If you are searching for the right community—or communities — and haven't yet found them, don't give up. They are out there for you. You'll just need to keep looking.

Keep this in mind, though: timing is everything. Just as it can be with dating, you might run into a community a few years after determining it wasn't for you only to find that you've had a shift in perspective. Perhaps you tried a chapter of a larger organization and didn't fit, but in another chapter, you feel right at home. Perhaps when you didn't connect one-on-one with someone the first time, you find more in common the second. Whatever the case is, it can take time and work to find the right set of roller coasters for you. When you do, make sure you stick with them.

There was no second date with "boring *Survivor*" guy. Not long after, I met my husband. Ironically, he had a weekly get-together with some of his neighbors to watch *Survivor*, and being a good sport, I started to watch too. It is now one of my favorite shows. Timing really is everything.

50

INTERNALIZE THIS SECTION

Sometimes it is extremely easy to develop the community we need. As a new mom, connecting with women in a new mothers' group was especially easy. There was an immediate bond based on our current shared experience. But when we strike out on our own doing something different, like building a business, when no one around us is doing the same, we can feel desperate for a community that understands.

As entrepreneurs, building a community is vital on so many levels: we need and want referrals, we want to market ourselves, we need people who understand us, we need people who will push us and support us. Here are some things to consider about yourself and the community you will need and want:

- Were you taught how to socialize and to develop healthy relationships? Is it something that comes easy or hard for you?
- Is there a particular group outside of entrepreneurship that has helped pave the way for you to grow and succeed?
- Have you found your tribe of roller coasters? Do you need to

create or expand one? What steps do you need to take to move that forward?

- What gaps are you not filling in your business? Are you trying to force yourself to fill them? Could you get support that would allow you to focus on your strengths?
- How do you nurture relationships? Do you have an active plan around doing so?
- How can you position yourself to give more than you look to get in your business connections?
- Are there individuals or groups that you just felt you didn't connect well with? Do you feel you've handled it effectively without letting it derail your progress?

LEADERSHIP

51

LEADERSHIP

 Leaders become great not because of their power but, because of their ability to empower others.

— JOHN MAXWELL

I have learned many lessons about leadership throughout my tenure as an entrepreneur. At the beginning of my journey, I wanted to jump in and become a business coach. Despite having an MBA in marketing and entrepreneurship, I didn't feel I could be a coach until I'd had my own successful business.

My solution was to create The Implementation Station, a virtual assistant business for entrepreneurs looking to build revenue online. My Implementation Station team and I added a lot of value for our clients. We helped them launch programs, kept them on track with consistent email outreach, updated websites, and created the materials for more online launches, tele-summits, and webinars than I can count.

Looking back, I learned a lot of lessons about leadership during The Implementation Station years. Some were because of successes, and some because of failures. There have been times I've chided myself for having a mindset that didn't believe a woman with an MBA in entrepreneurship had enough knowledge to be a business coach. Then I remember how much I learned creating that business from nothing, setting and hitting revenue goals, and building a team. I would not be the person I am today had The Implementation Station not existed. So instead of chiding myself, I choose to be grateful for the experience and the opportunities.

52

IT'S NOT ABOUT YOU

I remember overhearing conversations between my father and his friends where they called me a "natural born leader." I believe this was because I am outgoing, reasonably articulate, and comfortable with sharing my opinions. In the 1970s, these were characteristics men were not as used to seeing in young girls. Consequently, these traits made me stand out, and my father reinforced them in me by being entertained and charmed by them.

As a result, I saw myself as a leader. I don't recall feeling afraid to stand up and read, raise my hand to volunteer for something, or even to get up in front of people to perform. Each of these things came naturally to me. They still do.

What I didn't understand then was that these characteristics have very little to do with leadership. Leadership, in my opinion, is never a "natural born" characteristic, but rather a series of choices, actions, and attitudes that blend together to create a quality within someone that allows them to teach, encourage, and guide others to perform.

Throughout grade school and high school, because I thought of myself as a leader, I ran for and applied for positions I associated with leadership. I was a doer, a joiner, a get involved kind of girl. I made the cheerleading squad, and, by my senior year, I was one of the captains. I applied for Peer Group, and while I was cut in my junior year, I made it for senior year. I participated in the school theater program and was cast in every show I tried out for, receiving lead roles my senior year. I was even the co-editor of the school newspaper. Most of the time, managing all these responsibilities and commitments went just fine; therefore, it was easy for me to believe that participating in these endeavors showed leadership.

When I went to college, this pattern continued. I went to all the parties, got involved in a sorority, was cast in the plays I tried out for, and somehow landed a spot as a student representative to the Board of Trustees. For the life of me, I can't remember how that happened. What I do remember is applying to Omicron Delta Kappa (ODK), the leadership organization on campus, in spring of my junior year. I thought I was a shoe in.

ODK had an initiation ceremony on the steps of Richardson Hall, one of the oldest buildings on campus. Parents of new initiates were encouraged to surprise their student leader by revealing themselves at the top of the building's steps. Seeing one's parent showed new initiates they had been accepted into the elite group.

The morning of the ceremony, I made my way to the area of Richardson, and watched as other hopeful applicants arrived. I wondered if my mother, my father, or both would reveal themselves at the top of the stairs. I watched as parents came out to the top of the steps and one-by-one new initiates ran up to them for a hug. The group of accepted applicants swelled, and I waited, growing more anxious with each reveal. As the excitement seemed to peak, the announcement came, "Please welcome all of our new Omicron Delta Kappa initiates."

It was over—and I wasn't welcomed in. Despite all of my activities, the current members chose to exclude me from their ranks. One of my best friends, who also happened to be the ODK president, walked over to me, an expression of sympathy on her face. "I'm sorry I couldn't tell you," she said. She knew my expectations were dashed and that I was devastated.

It was the first time I realized being part of a lot of things didn't make me a leader. It made me a person who was willing to do a lot of different things. Thank goodness participation trophies weren't a thing back then. I would have needed a much larger dorm room!

Despite all that I did, I now realize I was still a follower, not a leader. I'd love to believe otherwise, but it wouldn't be true. Going back to my earlier statement, leaders teach, encourage, and guide others to perform. Like many who are young and finding their way in the world, I worried about my own performance and how it would be viewed and wasn't mature enough to realize the importance of reaching back to bring another along with me. I was worried, mostly, about myself.

This exemplifies for me one of the biggest lessons I've learned through my business: you are not a leader because of your own success; you are a leader when the success of those you lead is what shines.

It is easy to fall into the ego's trap of believing that your mark on the world comes from what you create for yourself. It doesn't. It comes from what you create for others, and how you help others create.

Imagine if Bill Gates had simply developed a software that allowed people to write content, manage numbers, and present electronically, but he and his team had never shown people how to communicate more efficiently and to build their businesses with it. I'm pretty confident he and Microsoft would not be the phenomenal success story they are. If Tony Robbins created programs that didn't impact people, he would not have his incredible following. He'd just be another life coach.

Similar to what I believed about my college activities early in my business, I made the mistake of thinking it was the actions I took that would make me a leader. What I've learned is that those actions, while critical to my success, are only a piece of the success puzzle. The rest of it is impact.

The breadth of our impact on someone we serve is the measurement we need to focus on as we create and develop our businesses. This is why casting your ego aside and focusing on service will help you build your business most quickly, and why it will have others calling you a leader long before you think you've earned that title.

I have learned that my own success is a function of how others prosper from our work together. My income is in direct correlation with how much my work is bringing tangible value to others. This is how it is, and how it should be. It's not about me.

53

MIDDLE OF THE NIGHT BUSINESS

O ne of the mistakes I've made is also one of the most common I see with other women business owners: charging too little for my services. During my early years in business, I spent way too much time on the phone with potential clients giving away my hard-earned knowledge for free. I also learned the hard way that charging too little when you are hoping to build your business is not the way to go.

Because of these mistakes, the first couple of years with The Implementation Station were extremely challenging. I traded dollars for hours, rather than creating a business that valued my expertise. Looking back, I know this is why I struggled to find good people to help me. I didn't charge enough, so I couldn't pay enough.

When I began my virtual assistant business, I asked for thirty dollars an hour. I was delighted when clients flooded in and I got busy in my business. I got the business to the point that I was making reasonable money as long as I did the work, but it couldn't compare to what I'd previously made in my corporate job. We were living in New Jersey and had a massive mortgage payment every month. Additionally, we were paying for nursery school. The pressure was enormous.

The increase in clients meant an increase in working hours, which quickly became unmanageable. Despite sending my boys to day-care several days a week, there never seemed to be enough hours in the day to get the work done. Often, I found myself working late into the night. In fact, I think I joined a culture of women entrepreneurs who built their businesses in the middle of the night!

One time in my first year of business, I struggled with a client's email system and just couldn't get an email to look right. I found myself mucking around in the code of her email marketing system, a place I knew just enough to be dangerous. At two or three in the morning, I finally had the email looking good and sent her a test. To my surprise, I heard right back from her. What followed was a lively exchange and some finishing touches to the email.

There was camaraderie knowing that some of my clients were hustling in their businesses just as much as I was. We balanced families, other jobs, spouses, and households. I loved supporting many of the women I did. Some remain friends to this day, and I have loved watching them grow over the past ten years. With certainty, I can say we'd all agree that we could have used a lot more sleep during that time.

The lack of sleep was a symptom, however, of what we were all doing. We gave so much of our time away for so little money, that we exhausted ourselves creating what we thought would be successful businesses. My friends and I all had to learn this for ourselves, sadly, through trial and error.

Initially, I enjoyed learning all the client systems and was happy to learn them "on my own time," but excitement and interest for that faded. What I really loved was marketing the businesses. Gradually, I recognized that I ought to focus on marketing and pass the hands-on work to others. I also learned I couldn't make any money and pay someone else if I only charged thirty dollars an hour. I felt as though I was in a vicious cycle and couldn't get out.

This cycle translated to stress in my household. Anyone who has been a parent knows the early years are challenging simply because of the level of attention young children need. I remember trying to be all things to all people. Often, when I arrived home after picking my boys up from preschool, I would realize that I couldn't remember the drive home. It was as though I was on autopilot. As you can imagine, consuming energy that way meant that I had very left over to be a loving wife.

The decision to charge more was obvious. Enacting it was a lot harder, especially because I knew I had to ask my largest client for a fifty percent increase in what she paid me. We had a wonderful relationship, and I was doing a great job for her, but anticipating asking for that kind of raise made me sick to my stomach. If she said no, I would lose a significant portion of my monthly income. If I didn't ask, I couldn't bring on help for her account and I knew I wouldn't be able to grow the business.

I'm grateful to this day for the value she saw in me. She agreed to the increase and remained a client. She worked with me so long she was the last virtual assistant client I had. We released each other when the time was mutually right. The many years we worked together are small in comparison to the friendship we built along the way.

Raising my prices to charge what I was worth, and to bring on the team I knew I needed, was a seminal moment for me—and for my business. In doing so, I showed myself how to lead my company.

Through doing so, I learned that as a business owner you always need to ask yourself if you are charging what you are worth, and if the offers you are making make sense. You need to understand your marketplace, where you fit in, and what people are willing to pay for your services. And, of course, you need to understand any costs before you price your service.

I'm not suggesting that you do cost-plus pricing, but you must have a sense of your profit margin before you go to market. It can't be a "we'll figure that out when we get to it" scenario. I consider myself extremely lucky that my major client valued me enough to give me the increase I asked for. I will never put myself in the position to need that kind of grace from a client again.

54

HURRICANE SANDY

I still remember a conversation I had with Donna, who coached virtual assistants in growing their businesses. We had met a week earlier in the lunch line at a women's entrepreneurial conference. I decided after that conference to create a virtual assistant business and I wanted to run some business names by her.

My vision, right from the start, was that I would begin by doing all the client work myself. Then, I would hire sub-contractors to do certain tasks. Donna's affirmation of The Implementation Station name was the first of many things she helped me with over the next number of years.

My plan required me to do two things I had little experience with in my corporate career: hire people and manage them. During my corporate years, I managed many projects that involved other people, requiring their buy-in, and setting expectations for them, but I never actually had a team that reported to me.

Within six months of starting my business, it was time for me to get some help. Donna taught me to hire slow and fire fast. In the first year of hiring sub-contractors, even when I had references, they often came and went quickly. Desperate for support and working too many hours, the hiring slow part of that equation didn't stick. Firing fast did though, especially when I was let down and had to pick up the pieces for a client, often at the expense of my sleep or sanity.

About a year and a half into the business, in the last few days of October 2012, three milestones converged. Hurricane Sandy crushed parts of New Jersey, where I lived at the time, my father succumbed to Alzheimer's disease, and Bernadette joined The Implementation Station team.

On a Friday afternoon, I was walking exhausted through Target pushing one of their large red carts. My boys, five and three, climbed in an out of it, grabbing things from shelves and begging to walk down the toy aisles.

Earlier that day, I had received a phone call from my mother, who was up in New Hampshire. "Suzie, I think this might really be it. The doctor is coming over, but from everything I've read, I think Daddy isn't going to last much longer." She described for me what was going on, and that I needed to decide if right then was the time to pack up the car and go say my goodbyes.

Strolling through Target, I was on the phone with a friend who owned an in-home care company. She and her husband had become adept at death and the conversations and decisions around it. While keeping my children from claiming every toy on the shelf, I discussed with Sarah how long, based on Mom's earlier description, my dad likely had to live. She confirmed that he was likely within a few days of completing his life. It was late in the day, so I made a plan to leave for New Hampshire the next day after Stuart's Saturday morning soccer game.

At that stage of my life, I rarely watched the news. So, the next morning at soccer was the first time I heard anything about the possibility of a hurricane hitting our area. All the soccer dads discussed running out that afternoon and buying generators. When Kevin suggested we might want one, I laughed at him. I reminded him that our power lines were underground and that in the seven years we'd lived in our townhouse we'd only lost power once, and then only for a few hours.

That weekend, I felt as though I was living in a haze. For days, I had been crying intermittently, anticipating the loss of my father. A hurricane seemed like a mirage in the distance I simply couldn't wrap my head around.

On the way home from soccer, my mom called again. "Dad seems to have perked up a bit. I don't think you need to rush up here."

I spent much of the rest of the day questioning what would be the right decision. I discussed with Kevin all the factors that were swirling in the mix—an impending hurricane, how to manage our children and dog, and whether or not we thought this was really the end. By the afternoon, I decided I was too physically and emotionally exhausted to make the trek to New Hampshire that night. I planned to leave in the morning.

Sunday morning, I packed up the children, the dog, and appropriate funeral clothing, and headed for New Hampshire. Kevin stayed behind expecting to go to work on Monday. About ninety minutes into the drive, Kevin called to tell me that his Manhattan office would be closed on Monday because of the anticipated storm. He packed up, and headed for New Hampshire as well, going first to his office to pick up his laptop.

I arrived at my parents and immediately spent some time with my father. I told him I loved him, that I knew he loved me, and that he had been a wonderful dad. He was conscious and able to respond to me although unable to speak. Unlike earlier visits when he seemed confused by his Alzheimer's, he appeared much more cogent to me. I don't know if this is truth, or a lie I tell myself, but I really felt he knew me, knew what I was saying, and was able to digest it. That night, he slipped into the space between life and death. He breathed but showed no signs of connecting with anything we said to him.

Monday, my brother, mother, and I moved in and out of my parents' bedroom, speaking to and about Dad, watching the coverage of Hurricane Sandy, and worrying about all of our friends in New Jersey. My sons came in and out of the room when they wanted to see me, sometimes they played on the Oriental rug in front of the fireplace, other times they simply observed, or came to get a hug.

At times, I had my laptop open and worked next to my dad. I had clients who were expecting work to be completed. That afternoon, I had an important phone call with Bernadette, the latest sub-contractor

I had hired. We were supposed to get her going on some projects. I told her where I was, what was going on, and asked that if I wasn't imme-diately responsive to please understand. I will always remember that in the conversation she said, "I just want to be a blessing to you, Suzanne." She was then, and for the following five and a half years. In truth, she still is today, just no longer as a work associate.

Together, we got through the death of my father later that week, and the two subsequent weeks I spent at my parent's house. Despite our underground power lines, our New Jersey home had no power for several days. Many in our area were without power for eleven days. School was closed for our boys for two weeks. The generator I'd laughed at Kevin about would have been very helpful.

In later years, Bern and I got through her sister's diagnosis of and passing from cancer, the death of her mother, and her own cancer diag-nosis. (Fortunately, she is healthy today and we are very much in touch.)

We also got through countless client issues. We supported each other. Talked each other "off the ledge" when needed and boosted each other up when necessary. Without question, my business never would have grown the way it did without Bernadette. She taught me what it was to guide someone while also being empathetic to their challenges. More importantly, she forgave me when I didn't get it right.

There were other women along the way who did a wonderful job for me, and I'm grateful to every single one of them. No one had the impact Bern did though, both on the business, and on my personal growth. People and relationships are critical to your business. Don't ever take them for granted.

55

OWN IT

One of the biggest lessons I learned running The Implementation Station, is that when you are the leader, you own every mistake. It didn't matter if I made it, if a team member made it, or if it was simply something lost in translation. I owned the mistakes. The process of learning this was not fun.

Many times, I've been asked why I gave up my virtual assistant business when it seemed like a money-maker. My answer is always the same, "It got really old feeling that I was only as good as the last email I sent without a bad link."

You have certainly experienced receiving an email only to have it followed shortly by another email with the subject line "CORRECTED LINK." Behind each one of those is a sender who has likely suffered an irrational amount of angst. If she had a virtual assistant who sent the email, the angst was multiplied.

Bad links, forgotten scheduling, missed assignments, not adhering to checklists, and even, one time, a link that took someone to a porn site because a client's website was corrupted, these were all just part of the business. The simple, human errors like those wore people down. As the leader of my company, I learned to take responsibility for all of them, a task I found it exhausting.

Responsibility looked different depending upon the issue, and whether or not the person on my team was a habitual offender. Sometimes I gave clients credit. Sometimes it was the last in a long line of challenges resulting from one of my team members and I let her go. Often my time following apologies to the client was spent speaking with a team member and reminding her that she's human; we all make mistakes!

One of my biggest areas of personal growth during this time was around displaying empathy. I had clients for whom a bad link felt as though it was monumental. I learned to put myself in their shoes and accept that their feelings were valid. Of course, sometimes I thought, "This was a pretty easy mistake to fix. Can we just move on?" But that thought didn't serve the client. My team and I were paid to make their lives easier, to get things right, and to add value to their businesses. When we didn't, it was a problem.

In the early days of my business, when I got off of a phone call with an angry client, I'd follow up with the team member right away. At times, I didn't show concern for the team member, instead my ego got the better of me. I felt so much pressure for my business to run well, that I didn't always comport myself ideally.

At that time, I didn't understand that showing my frustration at their errors was unproductive. What I learned was you never get the best from people when you make them feel bad. Honest criticism of their actions was reasonable and educational. Barking at them when still in a state of frustration wasn't.

Gradually, I learned that many of my team members felt it deeply when they made a mistake. They were emotionally invested in getting things right. They took it to heart when they didn't. I became more understanding when I understood that when they made a mistake, they felt crushed too.

I evolved into a more caring leader. I recognized that everyone in the ecosystem I developed worked hard to get things right. I began to pause between the angry client phone calls and team follow-ups, giving myself the chance to breathe and release my frustration so that I could hold space for my team member who often felt shattered by her mistake.

I learned that fully taking responsibility meant owning the entire situation. I didn't get to escape to my ego where I told myself the issues were someone else's fault. I didn't get to play the victim card and blame others, even in my own head.

My own frustrating mistakes came when I accepted clients that my gut told me I shouldn't. Always pushing to earn more, I sometimes took clients against my better judgement. It was a mistake every single time.

There was one that I will never forget. She hired our team to help her with a launch. She spoke to me intermittently about it for months, but, like so many, once she wanted to move forward, everything was a rush. She paid an initial deposit but then didn't keep up with benchmark invoices. When reminded about them, she indicated intent to get them paid through a team member, but the money didn't show up. I had long established upfront payments and payment benchmarks, but allowed my standards to slip, foolishly believing this client would pay because of mutual relationships. We were on a timeline for the launch, and I kept my team member working on the project so that we didn't fall behind.

The client's communication with me, and my team, was horrible. She didn't respond in a timely fashion, and when she did her feedback was laced with insults. I had to beg my team member to finish the project by promising her that she wouldn't have to speak directly to the client again. Rightfully, my team member didn't accept the client's verbal abuse.

There were several times that I should have walked away, but I just didn't. Oh boy, did I have to own that one. I sat one afternoon at a ski lodge, working while my children participated in an after school ski program when an email came. "Your team did a shitty job and I'm not paying you another dime!" My heart stopped. I owed my team member five times the amount of the client's initial deposit and had not received any other payment.

As a business owner, when you face a situation like this, you have to take responsibility for it. I had to take the time to unravel it and recognize where I went wrong. I could be angry with the client. I could be frustrated with the mistakes made by my team member; there were some. Ultimately though, I created the situation by lowering my standards. I allowed the mess to happen. I paid my team member and accepted the financial loss.

It was the last time I ever worked with a client who hadn't paid up front. I will never do so again. Now, I know I always must decide on standards and values for my business, and then I must live by them.

56

SQUIRRELS

One of the most challenging elements of leadership in my ten-year journey of entrepreneurship was staying focused on the one or two most important initiatives of the moment. The more laser focused I have been, the more success follows. Alternatively, when I spread myself too thin, both my finances and I were a mess.

No one can be successful if she tries to take advantage of all the opportunities around her, regardless of their qualities. I have been guilty too many times of believing I could take on, just one more thing.

Being a true lover of business, opportunity, and possibility has, at times, been my downfall. Whether it is a course, a mastermind, a new business tactic, or an entirely new business, the number of times I've followed that squirrel are countless.

"Hi, I'm Suzanne Moore. I am a marketing coach, I sell Rodan + Fields skincare, and I also help women ditch their bras for a more comfortable, yet still supportive, alternative."

As you might imagine, that elevator pitch did not get me a lot of business! Instead, it created confusion, and kept me from excellence at any one of those pursuits.

This experience was not unique to me. At countless networking meetings, as women introduce themselves, I marvel at how many companies they represent all at once. Occasionally, I find women who come up with one integrated message, brilliantly finding the link between all of the companies with which they've affiliated. Most of the time though, the pitches sound a lot like my own former hot mess message from above.

It is impossible to become a leader at anything when you are going in too many directions. Most women already spread themselves too thin, between business, family, household, friendships, and other responsibilities. Why do we think if we are not achieving great things in one business adding another is going to be the answer? Taking on more only holds us back.

When we struggle and aren't making the money we need or want, being wooed by the promise of easy sales is understandable. The more people we know in network marketing, the more often we hear those promises. It would be easy to blame the businesses that use this model for their ability to distract us. However, they are not to blame. I am a firm believer that they represent an amazing opportunity for millions of people around the world and that the stigma of "the pyramid scheme" needs to die. That said, I have allowed myself to get involved in one too many. Health drinks, water and air purifiers, essential oils, supplements, skin care, bra alternatives and active wear, you name it: I have been there and done that. Halting this behavior is one of the best things I've done to establish my role as a leader in my own business.

The other distraction I see is when entrepreneurs move from solution to solution, never giving the last one the time and attention necessary for success. It is very easy when you are not making enough income to be attracted to coaches and entities who tell you what they are selling will make all the difference for you. Often, they speak as though they are holding the "Holy Grail" in their hands.

In truth, if you've already invested in one "Holy Grail" solution and haven't given it the time, attention, and reworking it deserves, what they are holding is a squirrel who's movement in front of you is simply taking your attention off the task at hand. It will always feel easier to try a new tactic than to diagnose what is going wrong with the current one.

One of the best pieces of advice I can give any business owner, and

I know this all too well from personal experience, is to choose one path and make it your comprehensive focus. If you get bored, tired, or need to re-energize, decide how you can make that happen focusing on a single path. When you don't, you create confusion which keeps you from both success and leadership.

57

THE MESSAGE IN YOUR HEART

Entrepreneurs love learning. I believe this is why many of us end up as entrepreneurs. Learning about what we do. Learning how to do it better. Learning how to market our products or services better. Learning how to sell our stuff better. When I started my business, I was like a sponge who wanted to learn everything there was to know about online programs and how I could support entrepreneurs with them. If I didn't know a system, I spent hours playing with it or watching training videos so that I could support clients with it.

As I shifted into coaching, I wanted to learn more about the latest and greatest tactics to market myself. There was always someone out there to teach a new approach. I followed hundreds of other business and marketing coaches to see what they were doing and what methods they used. I wanted to understand the latest and greatest technology breakthroughs and how others were employing them.

Business is always changing and evolving. Online business does this at warp speed. As that is the playground I live in, I have exhausted myself watching coaches I admire pivoting, trying to keep up with every nuance. For a long time, I assumed that others knew more than me and that I had to keep learning everything they knew. If I wasn't up on the latest and greatest platform, I believed people would see me as a fraud.

There were some entrepreneurs I connected with who I felt were more successful than me. I watched them watch others, shifting their marketing language and offering new and different programs in order to keep up with the biggest names in coaching. It appeared to be the thing to do. I still see this today. A well-known coach finds a new way to market herself, and suddenly Facebook ads for people I've never heard of pop into my feed selling a similar system to the guru. Instead of a fad diet, we see a marketing fad. Ironically, the same message is shared by every marketing strategist I know: find what makes you unique. Yet struggling coaches find the fads instead.

I don't mean we can't shift our focus. Pivoting comes along with the territory of being a learner and a coach. We love to incorporate what we learn into what we teach. However, we can't look externally for our personal, unique message. It needs to come from within.

Watching others, held me back for ages. Finally, I saw a friend shift her business and thought, *this is good*. Jeannie and I met just before I started my virtual assistant business, which means we knew each other from the beginning of my entrepreneurial journey. We became friends and supported each other along the way. For a while, Jeannie was a virtual assistant client. Later, she was my coach. While not spending much time together over the years in person, we have been connected in many ways I am grateful for.

It always felt like Jeannie was a few steps ahead of me, but not so much that I found her intimidating. I have watched her transition from working on her business in addition to holding a full-time job, running her business in what she called "tiny pockets of time," to becoming a successful multi six-figure entrepreneur running a business she loves.

From my perspective, the shift that created her transition was not figuring out what someone bigger, better, or flashier was doing and emulating it. The shift came when she took all the hard-earned knowledge she'd earned and invested in for years and realized her own message within it.

In April 2016, about five years after we met, I attended an in-person workshop that Jeannie held in Providence, Rhode Island. The full day event focused on using speaking to create success in business. I knew Jeannie to be very bright and very articulate, but until then I didn't understand her ability to carry the energy of a room. Her passion, preparedness, hard work, and study shined across the room.

On that day in April, Jeannie became a teacher. Watching her transformation was one of the best lessons I've experienced for my business. It showed me that I needed to find my own message, rather than looking at someone else's and see how I could tweak it. Jeannie showed me that I needed to stake my claim about what I believe to be true about business and marketing. And then I needed to teach it to others.

This was a turning point for me. Others had told me to "trust my gut," my intuition. "Breathe and then take the next best step forward." All solid advice, and what I needed to hear, but I couldn't figure out how to apply it. Apparently, I needed to see it displayed for me, and that day, Jeannie showed me the exact path was the one I needed to create myself.

This is the path leaders take. They develop their unique message, their belief system, and then they figure out the best way to communicate it. They teach people how to apply it in their own businesses to affect desired change. Leaders have their own message. This is what makes them leaders, instead of followers.

Please don't think that I'm no longer a learner in my business. I continuously learn and grow. I can't imagine not doing so and fear I would become stagnant. But today, I know that all the following I did helped me to build my own path; following another person was never the way to leadership.

Rather than looking to someone else and saying, "I want to do what they do," learn what you can from them and apply that knowledge to the message that is in your heart. The one you know people need to hear from you. Then go share it.

58

REWARDS

I shared earlier that I believe leadership is about action and about creating value for others. A significant part of my perspective on this comes from my experience of developing and running a Polka Dot Powerhouse chapter. I walked into my first meeting ready to find a community and ready to start a community if I didn't find one. By a stroke of luck, I found I could do both and create something even more meaningful.

At the end of that first meeting, the chapter leader made a point to connect with me. "Do you think you might want to join us?" she asked.

"Oh, absolutely!" I responded. "What do I need to do to start a chapter?"

I explained that, while I would absolutely join her chapter, it was about an hour from my home without traffic. I wanted to create a chapter nearer to my home. Within a few hours, I had both become a member of the organization, and submitted an application to start a chapter.

Over the course of the next seven weeks, I interviewed with six leaders in the company, and did homework between each interview. Some homework included speaking with other Managing Directors, women who had recently been through the process of starting a chapter. I took copious notes, wrote summaries, and hoped to be welcomed into the next step of the process.

Then, I needed to find potential venues that would work with me to provide a comfortable location, reasonably priced meal, and separate checks for up to thirty-five attendees. It surprised me how difficult this was to do where I live.

As I passed through each phase of the application process, I marveled at the wisdom involved in the requirements for each step. Through each assignment, I learned more about the role I sought and the requirements of starting a chapter from scratch. The process impressed me and made the position more desirable the further I went. Not only was I looking forward to beginning a chapter, but I became excited to be a part of an organization that had such a smartly designed process. It was clear to me there would be more to learn with these women.

The final directive was to bring on two members within a window of time. I couldn't proceed to my final interview with the company founder, Shannon Crotty, until I had done so. I signed on three and scheduled my interview with Shannon for the following Friday morning. I wasn't sure what to expect when I logged into that Zoom call in early March 2019, but Shannon was warm and friendly. She put me at ease quickly and the conversation was comfortable. Toward the end of our hour together, she looked at me and said, "I don't always do this, but I feel really good about this, and I'd like to offer you the Managing Director position." Needless to say, I accepted.

Despite the work involved, I felt as though I had hit the jackpot. Not only had I found an amazing group of women whose gatherings fed my soul, but they helped me to position myself as a leader in my new area. When I reached out to women to share about the chapter I created, I was also able to tell them about the huge network they would get to be a part of if they joined. The whole thing was a win-win to me if ever there was one.

Looking back on it, I did hit the jackpot. Partly because of all the benefits above, but more importantly, I learned that an element of leadership was not letting yourself down. Prior to starting my chapter, there had been so many times I had let myself down. There were programs I wanted to create but never did, workshops I wanted to run, but chickened out of. I launched a podcast and after thirty episodes just stopped doing it. Starting my Polka Dot chapter was different. Failure was not an option.

If you've been in business a while, I'm sure you can relate to letting yourself down. I don't know an entrepreneur who can say that she's never let something get in the way of a goal she'd set for herself. This goal was mine, but others were invested in it, too. Emotionally, I knew if I let them down, I would never forgive myself.

Wisely, the leaders at Polka Dot provided incentives for hitting certain milestones in the launch and chapter building processes. We all love a good incentive, right? The first was to recruit enough members ahead of the launch event that the founder Shannon would come speak at it. The second was to recruit enough members within a reward year to earn a trip to Maui with the company.

Several chapter leaders in my area had earned both rewards when launching their chapters. The more I got to know these women, the more I respected them, and felt honored to be among them. They were all well-educated, high energy, smart, kind, and supportive. Together, they'd set a high bar, and showed me what was possible. I hustled harder to earn both of these incentives than I had hustled for anything before in my business. I needed to show myself that I could stand shoulder to shoulder with them as a leader.

I also hid the Maui incentive trip from Kevin. When I earned it, I delighted in telling him that we were going to Maui together the following fall. He has supported me for a long time in all of my entrepreneurial endeavors and it felt wonderful to surprise him with such a lovely reward.

Before starting the Polka Dot chapter, I thought the rewards for doing so would be different. I won't lie and say that my ego didn't love the idea of being "the leader." But the real benefits for me have been the lessons I needed in order to grow my business. I learned what it looks like to not let myself down in the process of actualizing something I'm trying to achieve. This is the best reward I ever could have received.

59

THE OXYMORON OF LEADERSHIP

It can be tempting to desire leader status. The best leaders make leading look easy. They arrive at podiums looking like they own them, sashay onto stages as though they have been doing so since birth and bring a message and value to those who will listen. From the outside looking in, leadership looks fun, commanding, and full of accolades.

In truth, leadership requires hard work, difficult decisions, and long hours. It can be fraught with guilt for making an error in judgment, or for letting those who follow you, in whatever way they do, down. It is anything but easy. Until you are a leader, you don't know the kind of energy, effort, focus and determination it takes.

It can also be lonely. Leaders, while at the center of the universes they create, can be the forgotten members of the tribe. They are set aside and held at arms-length. Assumptions are made that they are too busy to be a part of the hustle and bustle members of the group enjoy.

The oxymoron of leadership is that those of us who desire to be leaders can't truly understand this until we have achieved it. Don't take this to mean that I regret any bit of the leadership I have committed to and achieved. That is not the case at all. Especially as I now understand it is tied to the value I bring to others.

What I discovered through the process was that I need to also put myself in places where I am not leading, but where I get to be the learner or attendee. Having worked so hard to find myself leading rooms of people sometimes, I value more now the times I get to blend into the crowd, sending simple love and energy to the leader and recognizing this is her space.

60

INTERNALIZE THIS SECTION

Jack Welch said, "Before you are a leader, success is all about growing yourself. When you become a leader, success is all about growing others." No matter how you define leadership, it is part of being a business owner. Whether you are leading a solo enterprise or a large organization, many of the skills and values required are the same. Above all, your focus needs to be on bringing value to customers, because you succeed only by doing so.

Each of us needs to learn how to be an effective leader in our own way. We need to understand our skills, our education, and how to best use our energy. In doing so, we learn how to apply our knowledge in service to others.

- How do you define leadership? Do you feel you are living up to your own definition or are on the path toward it?
- Do you have a team that supports your business? Are you leading them well? Have you created an environment where they feel confident to step in and make decisions when you are not available?
- What is the worst decision you have had to own? How did doing so affect future decisions?

- Do you allow yourself to be dragged off course by "opportunities" that don't support your larger vision?
- Are you an avid learner? Have you been able to synthesize your learning into a message of your own?
- Do you let yourself down in ways you would never let others down? How can you create supports in your business to keep yourself from doing so in the future?
- Have you ever experienced the lonely part of leadership? What do you do to get beyond it or to accept it?

CELEBRATE

61

CELEBRATE

 Celebrate what you want to see more of.

— Thomas J. Peters

One of the things we women are not so great at is celebrating our accomplishments. I find this to be true of almost all women, and doubly true of entrepreneurs. When we are driven, we tend to focus on the next step, the next achievement, the next challenge. There is nothing wrong with setting our sights high, but if we never take the time to pause and reflect on our triumphs, we miss out on all the good that comes from doing so.

In Polka Dot Powerhouse meetings, leaders invite everyone gathered to share a celebration. Often, I hear about the achievements of children or grandchildren, rather than women who claim that moment to celebrate their own accomplishment. There is nothing wrong, of course, with celebrating a son's graduation or the announcement a new grandchild is on the way, but I always wonder what that woman has achieved for herself recently that she is allowing to be over-shadowed.

62

FEEL THE WINS

A chievements themselves can be inherently draining. Taking the time to celebrate your accomplishments, to deeply feel the satisfaction of the work that you have done is energizing. Clients and mentors I've worked with throughout the years have shared how exhausted they are at the end of running a multi-day retreat. The wisest ones build recovery and celebration time into the planning.

My personal experience is that running even short events can be draining. Running them and turning immediately to the next project or the follow-up is demoralizing. Roller coasters would not be as fun if the highs didn't exist. That's where the exhilaration comes from, and why people love to get back on them. But after every high comes a swoop downward and what you choose to do with that can make a big difference on your ability to build up to the next high. If you're not celebrating, you are missing out on the best part of all of your hard work: taking pride in and feeling your accomplishment.

When you take the time to celebrate, it raises your vibration. And remember from the mindset chapter, when you raise your energy, you attract more of what you want.

Conversely, when you don't take time to celebrate, you cut off the flow of energy you've worked hard to create. It can be hard to believe, but celebrating your wins actually helps you to create more of them.

Before I understood this, when I signed a new client, I often responded in my head thinking, "Well that's good, but I really need two more this month for my income to be where I want it to be." This meant that I didn't feel the excitement I could have felt and didn't get energized by the process of signing a new client. It was not the only reason I struggled to sign clients, but I am certain it was a contributing factor.

Another contributing factor was that I'd spend a lot of time focused on what went wrong. There weren't enough clients, the client signed for three months instead of six. I got two clients from a webinar instead of nailing my goal of five. Instead of focusing on my success, I placed my energy on what wasn't working. As a result, I got more of what wasn't working. In every achievement there are challenges, things that didn't go quite right or as well as they could. We are wired to see those things and forget the good stuff. Sound familiar at all?

Today, I've learned to be excited now with every new client signed: to celebrate it, even if doing so alone. "Good job!" I tell myself. "Way to go! She's going to be an awesome client!" I congratulate myself whether the client is the first one in the month, or the one that allows me to hit a specific goal. I try hard to remember that every single small achievement adds up, and by celebrating and being grateful for each one, I am opening myself up to more.

I mentioned in the Mindset chapter how closely tied gratitude and forgiveness are. Celebrating is really a way of showing gratitude. To yourself, to your client, to your ability to achieve whatever it is you've been able to achieve. Doing so is showing that you forgive yourself for any of the small, or large, things that didn't go right along the way. There is power in it, but only if you allow yourself to feel it.

63

CLAIM YOUR GIFTS

We all know them: women who receive compliments by suggesting their achievement wasn't really theirs, their outfit isn't really special, or their exquisite dinner was simply a collection of recipes.

Many of us are these women. We've been taught the skill of deflecting deserved praise since we were little girls, most likely by our mothers and grandmothers, usually the women we admire most. Deflection was reinforced by those around us today, each of whom has been taught the same lessons: accepting praise was egotistical, stating what you are good at might make others feel bad, and if you can see what's wrong with it, so can everyone else.

These well practiced responses became like muscles developed over time based on bad posture. In order to correct them, they need to be retrained. It's more difficult than if they had been developed right the first time.

When I wrote about leadership earlier in the book, I shared my thoughts that leadership is not about you or me. It is about the value that we bring to others. Claiming our gifts is not about us either. It is about those who watch us do so gracefully and learn it is okay to do the same. Doing so enables us to spread our ripple effect beyond those we work with, or with whom they work.

I love watching other women achieve successes, telling them how great they are, and nudging them forward. One of the most fun things I've done in the last ten years was host a podcast because it provided me a platform to hold other women up and show off what they were doing. So often, I've seen them downplay their moment. This behavior does not serve them, and it does not serve those that follow.

In a period of tremendous turmoil, the United States recently saw the first woman sworn in as the vice president. Just before the inauguration, Kamala Harris was interviewed and shared that despite the challenges faced by the new administration, she was not going to let anything spoil her excitement for breaking that barrier. It was extremely important for her to celebrate that moment, to fully step into being the first woman, first African American—first Asian American—woman in that role. By doing so, she gave others permission to celebrate. If Vice President Harris had chosen to downplay that moment, it would have suggested that others who break barriers do not deserve to be recognized or to celebrate, extending the lessons of the past that belie something wrong with these behaviors.

Choose to be a woman who claims her gifts. When you do, you will show others it's okay to do the same. Perhaps one day we will no longer need to tell little girls everywhere to accept the praise heaped upon them, rather than deflecting it.

64

INTERNALIZE THIS SECTION

When Brandi Chastain whipped off her shirt to reveal her sports bra in celebration of her team's victory at the 1999 FIFA Women's World Cup, she showed women around the world what unfiltered celebration looks like. Imagine for a moment that you allowed yourself to feel your own unfiltered excitement. I'm not suggesting you disrobe in a coffee shop after the successful closing of a client over Zoom, but what if you allowed yourself, just for a moment, to really celebrate your victory.

Consider how sharing about a victory and showing your excitement, would impact others. Would it draw them to you, because they would see your success and want a piece of it? Would it show potential clients your appreciation for each and every person who works with you or buys from you? Might it make them feel even better about their decision to work with you? Would it make others feel the freedom to celebrate too?

Let's develop your celebration muscle!

- How can you begin to train yourself to develop your own version of unfiltered celebration?
- What holds you back from celebrating now?

- When offered a complement, how do you typically respond? Do you accept it graciously or do you deflect it?
- After reading this chapter, do you understand the connection between celebrating your successes and energetically attracting more of what you want?
- How do you think your clients or customers would respond if they saw you celebrate their investment with you?
- What were you shown about celebrating by those who raised you?

AFTERWORD

As a mother, a wife, and an entrepreneur, I've faced many challenges. No doubt, I will face many more. What I find fascinating after sharing my stories, strategies, and words of wisdom in this book is how much of overcoming every challenge happened between my two ears, right inside my own head.

We all have within us the capability to achieve whatever we want. We already know our own truths:

- That often we are acting—or not—due to fear;
- That sometimes we need validation to take action;
- That we get swayed or give up because we thought running a business would be easier;
- That there are days we need a shoulder to cry on and a great big hug;
- That most of the time we are doing our best to lead but wonder if anyone is going to follow; and
- That celebrating is scary because we're never sure we'll get to do it again.

Success is not a number. It is a feeling. You will not have it because you've hit six-figures, or enrolled twenty-five clients, or hired your first full-time employee —at least not long-term. Success is the quiet satisfaction within you that today you gave your best and that you are serving others.

It is my deepest wish that anyone who has come to the end of this book will not only find this kind of success but will do so while being more accepting of herself and where she is. I encourage you to strive for all you can think to achieve, but I want you to know that this looks different and happens differently for everyone. You are on your own roller coaster. Enjoy the ride!

ACKNOWLEDGMENTS

In addition to dedicating this book to my family, I must thank Kevin, Stuart, and Walter for supporting me throughout the writing process, which occurred when we were all spending a lot of time together at home. Without their understanding, I never would have finished it.

I thank Mom and Dad, too. There is so much of each of them throughout these pages. That is because of the richness of our lives and the closeness I feel to both of them. I am blessed to be their daughter.

If riches were measured in friends, I would be an extremely wealthy woman. So many have shown tremendous support about this book–and many of my other adventures! Thanks, and love to each of you. There are two I must specifically acknowledge: Anne and Wendy. The two of you are the ones who keep calling even when I don't. You are my greatest and most consistent supporters. My life would not be the same without you in it.

I write a great deal about Polka Dot Powerhouse. Shannon Crotty, thank you for starting this organization and for your leadership of it. You and the other leaders have helped me to grow as a woman, a business owner, and a leader. And I love the sisters who surround me. Special kudos to the women I masterminded with between September 2020 and June 2021.

To the members of Virtual Networkers, and our fearless leader Jill Celeste, thank you for the weekly love and support. You have lifted me up and made me feel connected and understood. Special thanks to Connie Jo Miller for keeping my books lemony-fresh; working with you makes me strive for more.

As I wrote this book, I reviewed the impact many people have had on me and on my business trajectory. Bernadette Raftery, you are an exceptionally special person. The years of work and learning together we experienced helped make me who I am today. Thank you for always being a blessing to me.

Fabienne and Derek Fredrickson, your work has made an immeasurable difference in my life. I'm grateful for every moment I've spent learning from you, and every investment I made. Thank you.

The best decision I made about a month into writing, was choosing my publisher. This book would not have come to fruition without the guidance and support of Debby Kevin and her brainchild, Highlander Press. As a girl who has felt that she has to do so much by herself in life, I am extremely grateful that I passed the reigns to Debby for the editing and publishing of this book. Thank you, Debby, for your love, support, and cheerleading. You, and the fall 2021 cohort of authors will always have an extremely special place in my heart.

RESOURCES

While I've learned this mostly through second-hand sources and through the reading of the book *Ask and It is Given: Learning to Manifest Your Desires* by Esther and Jerry Hicks, I believe Abraham-Hicks is foundation source of all that I am summarizing for you here.

"Abraham-Hicks." Home of Abraham-Hicks Law of Attraction, July 27, 2021. https://www.abraham-hicks.com/.

"Discover How to Improve Your Life." The Law of Attraction, June 1, 2021. https://www.thelawofattraction.com/.

"Help Them Know That Anything Is Possible... One Story at a Time." Adventures in Wisdom. https://adventuresinwisdom.com/.

"Mental Floss." Mental Floss. https://www.mentalfloss.com/.

"National Science Foundation - Where Discoveries Begin." NSF. Accessed August 9, 2021. https://www.nsf.gov/.

Sinek, Simon. "How Great Leaders Inspire Action." TED. https://www.ted.com/talks/simon_sinek_how_great_leaders_inspire_action.

Sinek, Simon. *Start with Why: How Great Leaders Inspire Everyone to Take Action*. East Rutherford: Portfolio/Penguin, 2011.

"What Are Thoughts & Emotions?" Taking Charge of Your Health & Wellbeing. https://www.takingcharge.csh.umn.edu/what-are-thoughts-emotions.

ABOUT THE AUTHOR

Photo credit: Jane Repetti Chang Photography

Suzanne Tregenza Moore knows all-to-well how living the entrepreneurial roller coaster feels. She's committed to stop women from playing Whack-a-Mole with To-Do lists while instead focusing on bringing revenue into their businesses using strategy, marketing, technology, delegation, and mindset. Her clients describe her as "invaluable," a "gentle butt-kick-er," and say she's helped them to "unleash their vision." A Jersey girl, born and bred, Suzanne and her husband Kevin now call the South Shore of Massachusetts home with their two sons and mini-labradoodle daughter named Lily. *Hang on Tight!* is her first book.

    facebook.com/suzannetmoore
    twitter.com/SuzanneTMoore
    instagram.com/suzannetmoore
    linkedin.com/in/suzannetregenzamoore

ABOUT THE PUBLISHER

Highlander Press, founded in 2019, is a mid-sized publishing company committed to diversity and sharing big ideas that change the world.

Highlander Press guides authors from where they are in the writing-editing-publishing process to where they have an impactful book of which they are proud, making a long-time dream come true. Having authored a book improves your confidence, helps create clarity, and ensures that you claim your expertise.

What makes Highlander Press unique is its business model focuses on building strong relationships and collaborating with women-owned businesses, which specialize in some aspect of the publishing industry, such as graphic design, book marketing, book launching, copyrights, and publicity. The mantra "a rising tide lifts all boats" is one Highlander Press embraces.

facebook.com/highlanderpress

instagram.com/highlanderpress

linkedin.com/in/highlanderpress

IF YOU LIKED THIS BOOK

You'll love the accompanying workbook, which you can download for free at https://suzannetmoore.com/hotworkbook.

Made in the USA
Middletown, DE
15 September 2021